AMERICA'S MASSACRE

THE SEQUEL

SURVIVING MASS INCARCERATION

TEWHAN BUTLER

INTERSTATE
NKMANSHIP
PUBLISHING

Acknowledgment

To my father, YahYah, may you rest in peace. I miss you.

To my loving mother, Pamela, who walks alongside me as I inch towards freedom.

To my nephew, Quanir, and my cousin, Sheyeast, thank you.

To the Butlers, Smiths and Swineys, thank you.

To my children Tewhan Jr. and Zamel; I love you. My gem, Della, your presence has transformed my lost journey into a voyage of purpose.

To Ak, Beast, Big Red, Beezo, Cory Grant, Grape Fats, H.B., Itchie Mu, Niki Hall, Ohs, Pito, Tia Ryans, Tommy Thompson, Quadree Smith, Q.B and All the men and women locked behind bars. In your own unique ways you all have contributed to the awakening of this project.

Special thanks to C. Orville McLeish of HCP Book Publishing for the great job he did with editing. Also, Sonya Meadows, for making the connection.

I want to make waves for all my Queen Street brothers and sisters; know that time and distance has not altered the love.

Introduction

Dear Tee,

As I lay here thinking of you on your birthday, I wonder how it must feel to celebrate it there. After talking to Aunt Pam about you a few minutes ago, I still find myself feeling pained and hurt. I don't know if I'm stuck on family and trying to keep everyone together or if it's the feeling of losing someone you care about so much, that it seems like a death occurred and the pain never goes away.

I have written you a million letters over the years, all unfinished and at a loss for words. I was afraid that I may say the wrong thing or the connection and bond we once had was gone. I don't have an opinion on what became of it, or you. I just feel like we lost each other in the process. No matter what road we took, I felt like we should have stayed close and been there for each other. There were times that I needed you, and for that, I was kind of angry with you. At the end of the day, I never stopped loving you.

I do hope we can work on rebuilding our relationship and move forward. There is so much I would like to talk to you about, get your advice on, hear your thoughts, and vice versa. We have missed too much time already. The walls can't stop us from continuing where we left off. So let me apologize for taking so long since our last letters to write again. My emotions get the best of me every time I start writing a letter to you. You being there doesn't mean that you can't still be a part of my life and me in yours.

I do hope our prayers for you have kept you mentally and emotionally stable. So how is it there? I mean, I hear how it is, but I would love to know how you survive prison. I can only imagine.

Take care and I love you.
Your Cousin,
Sheyeast

America's Massacre
The Sequel

Surviving Mass Incarceration

The pain of prison persisted as the suffering was less visible. It was not subjected to those who were not caged in this shell of darkness. There was a distance between the exuberant energies experienced '*socially*' and the fading hope of this caged community of non-persons. Considerably immoral was the dismissal of our free world. It didn't touch home and no one answered the door. Abandoned on the outskirts, we were deemed society's outcast; the 2.2 million blacks, browns, and Caucasians. So why did such suffering fall on the deaf ears of the many who claimed to hear well? Why did it remain unseen by the professed all seeing, and continued to go unfelt by the emotionally intelligent?

Was there not a human side to what we categorized as criminality? Did crime suggest we justified the dehumanization of our own? Was it that once shackled, it was the end of innocence as we knew it? Orphaning such individuals became simple, for they were not like us. The reality of prison couldn't be avoided. It must be confronted and approached with a sense of urgency, but more importantly, reached with that of compassion. One who had the desire to rehabilitate people, even if done in a prison setting, must possess, at the minimum, a genuine concern opposed to a calloused heart.

Prison as punishment under the guise of '*correction*' would forever lack true benefit. The quieted persons on the outside made way for such errored ways. Silence signified approval. Change was a global responsibility. Uplifting America's bottom half was not a case of particulars, but a righteous act to be carried out by all.

Let us not dismiss Matthew 25:45, *"That which you have not done for the least of man you have not done for me."* Leave us not behind; award us the true journey of life and the gift of redemption. Our flaws could once again be made precious, if only you would take us with you.

Chapter 1

New Beginnings

As I walked through the valley of the shadow of death, my new beginning began to feel more like the same old song: prison or death. A reality shaped by the darkest of truths woke me up to the systematic duties of our beloved country; a country that gave praise to mass incarceration. During my time spent on this earth, I had survived a number of intended deaths. The streets took no prisoners; yet here I stood, imprisoned by the American criminal justice system.

Fall 2007, November to be exact, I was removed from the unshakeable darkness of the New Jersey State Prison (NJSP) Management Control Unit, handed over to Federal Authorities and placed within a black hole (Federal Penitentiary). This was a captive's casket, where they trapped me in hopes of laying me to rest. For the majority of my previous five years spent in prison, not only had I been locked up, I had also been locked down. I was confined to a place we called, *'a prison inside of prison'*. It was a pitch black immeasurable hole with no light and very little hope; a psychological torture chamber.

The Management Control Unit inside NJSP was like no other. There was only one in the entire state of New Jersey, adjacent to the states infamous death row: the last stop, as they would say, your final destination next door. A surreal reality coming so close to death; a place where murder was legal. The Management Control Unit shared with death row the ill effects of one's last days. So when September 30, 2007 arrived, and I had maxed out my five year state prison term, an ecstatic feeling overcame me, contrary to the fact that I would only be beginning a thirty year federal term.

Upon my arrival at United States Penitentiary (USP) *'Big Sandy'*, a level six penitentiary deemed the worst of the worst, I readied myself for danger. A level six penitentiary on a scale of 1-10 in relation to its violent nature was a 12. Men fought little, attempted to kill almost always, and the staff was blatant with their prejudice. Consequently, depending on which angle you viewed your span of incarceration, the prison was left to be run by the inmates. The near unobstructed operation of the prison was what made *'Big Sandy'* such a threat.

A hurried conclusion did not take long. Although the severity of the existing dangers differed drastically, there was no denying the fact that we were in direct contact with danger. Opposed to state prison there were few friends, counterparts or associates. The pool of potential enemies stretched throughout the system and the system ranged from state to state. In the Feds, friends became overnight enemies, enemies turned into friends, and circles eliminated squares. The code was one way and those who violated the code got boxed up.

Here was where men convicted of some of the most unimaginable crimes called home. Your neighborhood reputation was irrelevant. The higher your 'street rep', the higher the chances someone was going to *'try'* you. A name worthy of esteem only placed a larger target on your back. No man was safe. The Federal Penitentiary was state prison amplified. The psychological and physical dangers were both high strung. Therefore the Feds called for craftiness, as though the danger of being in prison surrounded by men who lacked understanding did not suffice the ever present truth; the truth that these walls were created by over four hundred years of hatred. History's hidden hardships were upgraded to fit the times like fitted tees, and skinny jeans. A world fit into its self. What happened here, no one could fathom.

Although this was far from my first day in the midst of madness, this was my first day in the depths of darkness. What was to be expected was the unexpected. If the Federal Penitentiary was anything close to what I had heard *(tennis courts, swimming pools, and golf courses)*, then the Feds was similar to a caged amusement park, all things considered. Then again, one should believe none of what they hear, and half of what they see. So, for some strange reason, maybe the rapid pace of my heartbeat or the perspiration in my palms, there was a clear indication that where I was now was something else altogether. The void of these false luxuries was not the tell all.

The ailing expression on each man's face revealed even more the true nature of this place; a story of horrific pain and loneliness. Everyone in the prison looked angry. Yet, as my time came, I learned that anger was but a conjured emotion to shield the suffering that accompanied fear. Sadly, the love had been lost with the many souls that vanished.

Prison was actually filled with frightened men; men who grew up afraid. Afraid of a system which undoubtedly reared its ugly head whenever one seemed to get ahead. A system which told us at a tender age that we would only measure up by jumping through hoops and being twice as good. As we were educated on our A, B, C's and 1, 2, 3's, we were also being told that we were endangered. Too young to properly spell our names, yet statistics were already being tallied, proving that one in every three young black men would not only visit the inside of a prison, but become a resident.

The mean mugs and renewed 80's B-Boy stances inside the prison yard were all tactics to conceal just how afraid we actually were. We were afraid of how growing up without a father would affect our children. Afraid because although we felt the women we loved, loved us in turn, we knew love was not enough to keep the bed warm during those winter nights. We were not so much afraid of the uniformed officers as opposed to what those uniforms represented to an impoverished people. We were frightened because loneliness victimized all who came in contact with it and, as we know, victims tend to victimize others. From afar you would believe we were all fearless, courageous, warriors. In part we were, however, on the other side stood terrified sons, fathers, and brothers. Let us not forget the daughters, mothers, and sisters.

Men too hardened to smile were foiled by the fact that they were the *'living dead'*. They were crushed by a truth that many here were mourned by none; nothing more than forgotten corpses. The suffering endured, screaming of the mournful, deserted days, fiendish nights, and daunting dawns. Trapped in the twilight zone with time; stuck!

No man dared to venture into the wilderness of his own free will. Unfortunately, the feeling of freedom was unknown to many here. Freedom had never been theirs completely. Since birth, their existence had been a confined one; born into something identical to slavery, for reasons beyond one's grasp. Communities made like prisons with invisible ceilings and bars.

Along with the certificates of birth were reserved registration numbers (prison numbers). Inmate number 26852-050! Confined by way of society's expectations. Expectations such as rapping on a microphone, extraordinary athleticism, where one dunks like Jordan or dribbles like Irving, as well as cultural and class betrayal, were all society's derailments. To keep us asleep, they auto tune melodies softened with cars, clothes, and fast cash. This enslaved us mentally while erecting ideas of consumption and making us believe this was the only avenue to attain success. They partnered with our very own leaders, shackling the inevitability of advancement, and betraying the people.

"Many of these leaders are people who knocked their fathers off the stage, but won't let their sons or daughters get on." -Marc Lamont Hill

Poverty, self hate, individualism, and materialism were all forms of prison minus the bars. Lower class jailed, development arrested, and physically chained; prison was a likely bottom line. The initial gearing of mass incarceration was set in motion by disastrous particulars: economically disadvantaged neighborhoods; grossly ineffective school systems; high rates of crime; and don't forget their infamous drug funneling into urban communities.

This was the ugliness purposely put in place to reach exactly what was today a quiet more sophisticated holocaust. A beyond tragic event where the Nazi regime, under Adolph Hitler, habitually murdered an estimated 6 million Jews, including nearly half who died in death camps (prisons). What was different in the present? Only the air in which these murders were committed differed. In America the number of the fallen were rapidly growing. Save for bomb assaults, rifles, and hand grenades, there was the existence of slanted laws and steel cages. A steeled cage was the description we were fed as the appearance of prison. Yet, a better look provided a college campus structure with little education.

The inside was a mazed dungeon. The inner décor of walls and halls were a polished bright white and cemented grey. Yet nothing I had ever seen appeared so dark. Prison was on fire, just as hell was hot and run by devilish intent. The minds of the men charged by subjugation were run by fantasies of painting men as 3/5's human. This luxurious way of living was afforded through oppression and preying on the bodies of somebody until they become a nobody. How would this bid affect me?

Four years had passed since I was among the general population. For four years with the best of me, I survived debasement - snared in the stomach of nowhere. My chamber of death was dark like the city of Thebes, condemned by Zeus. For four years I rested without peace inside a stoned tomb. A castaway left to be lost to all the world. Although today I was not in the least bit safe from this warped seclusion, having the opportunity to walk around minus the chains and multiple officer escorts, left me cheering on the inside like a Nets crowd in Brooklyn's Barclay center. Yet, there was nothing to celebrate, for in prison was where I remained.

The conditioned freedom was both pleasing and patronizing. I had spent in excess of twelve seasons, multiple springs, summers, falls, and winters trapped, missing the magnificent manifestations of nature's transformation. Truths that man, along with each season, can be born again, rising from one stage to another. While each of these seasons were passing me by, I was lying dormant in the stillness of the winter. The blossoming promise of spring evaded me. Summer's full bloom was distanced, removed from physical contact. I was apart from all humanity. This sudden interaction with others left me both smiling and sweating in the middle of November. Twenty four hours passed and my first run in with a rival gang member ensued. Fortunately, the outcome was peaceful and eye opening.

****

Unexpected words were delivered by a rival gang member from New Jersey. I had been warring with this member since the day the Watts Grape Street Gang made its way into Essex County and the surrounding area. The message was for me to meet him in the prison yard at 9:00 a.m. In my mind, I thought, *"What could this guy possibly want with me?"*

Where I was from, the Bloods and Crips did no talking. Things were simple - on sight, bust first, no need for questions. So, why would he give me a heads up by sending me a message? The moment was beginning to take on the feel of school days when you sat quietly anticipating the outcome that waited when the clock struck three. The difference here, there would be no fisticuffs. Fights without weapons in the penitentiary were unheard of. Clearly, there were shanks (prison made knives), and a fight for one's life. To survive the scandalous ways of the streets, only to lose in the pen would be a hell of a thing. No way!

Avoiding the issue was out of the question. So I strapped up and made my way to the prison yard. My mind was made up to jump at the slightest move. I had my shoestring tightly wrapped around my wrist and my ice pick in a firm grip. It was do or die!

The metal detector guarding the yard entrance rung as I attempted to keep my cool and casually strolled out as if my heart was not racing a million miles an hour. My adrenaline was revved: kill or be killed! A new life with a new beginning would be over and done with as a result of a past I could not shake.

Slowly motioning around the track, hands concealed, spot on, eyes locked, *"What was running through his mind?"* I wondered. No crowd and no gang. It was just him and me. Certainly he was strapped. His reputation preceded him. This would be no easy feat. However, neither would I fall short. My gang and his neighborhood, with no knowledge as to why, other than colors, would forever be pitted against one another. I approached and he spoke. Already the unimaginable was happening. What was discussed shall remain between us two men. Not gangstas or gang bangas, but men. Years of misunderstandings, shootings, stabbings, and senseless killing, all overcome by the struggle. On this side of the wall our fight was the same. Our stories understood. This was the day that opened my eyes.

Nevertheless, when things calmed I discovered myself sitting outside on the prison yard conversing with five of my many co-defendants (Beezo, Death Blood, Drop G, Fox, and X-Blood); all of whom had arrived at the prison a few months prior. While recounting the events which shaped our lives, I began to unravel, recognizing the damage that had assaulted my psyche during my stay in solitary confinement. Hints of dementia were peeking through. *(People with a serious mental illness make up about 4% of the US's adult population, but count for 24% of jail inmates).*

General population or the Hole? Day Room or the Rec Yard? It was all designed to spawn submission. *"I can't let them break me,"* was what I told myself. However, I could not escape the piercing pain. I had been psychologically wounded, whether I chose to admit it or not. In spite of putting up my bravest attempt at overcoming prison and its ill effects, it still did something to all. The system's most particular objective was to crush man's confidence and curtail rebellious behavior. This was war. War as explained to me by a solid female comrade.

In my fight to not be dominated by a system which oppressed all who entered its doors, I had been scarred. During the conversation with my co-defendants, I noticed my senses red lining. I listened not only to what each of my co-defendants were saying, I also listened to every sound. I wanted to touch nothing. My eyes raced back and forth. My appetite was non-existent and, worst of all, I smelled death. The same stench that greeted me when I was led into New Jersey State Prison. I surmised that it was blood and guts, slain men, grim reapers and burial plots that rested just beneath the surface of all cinder blocked penal institutions.

My inability to socialize without being distracted troubled me. In the immediate presence of men I grew up with, I found myself more distracted by the misaligned motions of the general population. Like I-95, men rushed to and from different locations. Just about everyone appeared to be in a hurry, headed nowhere fast, or so I thought.

Further along into my prison term when I asked an older inmate, "Why the rush?" He replied, "When shit hits the fan, it's best to be either in the front or the back, but never in the middle." Then it all made sense. To be trapped in the middle of a violent outbreak was certain death. There was no way to determine where the next blow would come from. This I understood, but did not see until shortly after my departure from the Rec Yard.

Chapter 2

Violence Begets Violence

The walk from the Rec Yard back to the Unit gifted me with a sense of relief. Present in the yard was death, looming all around as you were viewed with suspicion. Who was armed? Who was having a bad day or just looking to fuck up another man's bid? Nearly all were angry at the state of their own reality. Such misguided anger, in large part, was the cause of many fallen men left dead on the prison yard.

Once back on the Unit, it was only a few short minutes before my Unit Officer yelled, "Mainline!" Unbeknown to me, the menu held something far worse than the usual slop served Monday through to Sunday. Today there would be two hungry men feeding on flesh.

Not alone, a comrade and I followed the prison's pace and began making our way to the dining hall. The Chow Hall was where I was to meet the remaining homies (bloods) who flooded the compound. This meet and greet was a new arrival requirement. A process conducted amongst inmates in which the new arrivals were virtually assessed, schemingly interrogated, and aggressively sized up. Not fitting the bill meant an immediate vote for you off the island, willingly or forcefully.

Over the years I would hear men speak of how they would not go *'up top'* (protective custody) for nobody, or how they weren't *'ducking no rec'* (avoiding confrontation), until these particular instances. Then fear would cover their faces as they took the long walk of shame, one against all.

It was inches in front of me, although I was not as attentive as I liked to be. A few feet away from the dining hall entrance, I felt my comrades flattened palm hit my chest, signaling me to stop. Two convicts in prison garb (beige khakis and black work boots) quickly approached one another. In slow motion, fluid and determined, there was one knife, then two. Like wild dogs with touching ribs they attacked.

There was a swift thrust, calculated chaos, bloodshot eyes, all awkward and calm. "Killers, kill! This was 1st degree." I thought. Each blow was snatching his breath away and he was too weak to

15

fight off his attackers. Hands, arms, and faces were covered in blood. Nearing, I heard the loud sound of jingling keys, and walkie talkies.

"Stop! Stop!" yelled approaching officers.

Pleading from a distance, the officers were too afraid to risk their own lives. Maybe prayer would suffice. Sacrificing self to save a convicted felon was no honorable death in their eyes. Vows and pledges were dismissed. We were no longer viewed as a part of humanity. The pleading was unheard and the attackers were deaf. They were wrapped in their mission. Kill! Nothing else mattered but what they came to do. A life with faded hope feels little. In his eyes, he had already been declared deceased. The gruesome display of murder continued. Chest were heaving and arms were flailing. The man lying across the corridor floor appeared lifeless. Inmates and C.O's alike were spectators to one of prison's damning effects; violent behavior. The men were cuffed and led away and the dead were placed on a stretcher and carted off. Two worlds meeting at once.

"Lockdown! Lockdown!"

The roaring calls by staff released me from my stupor. Shaking it off just in time to see C.O's lining the corridor walls, preparing to conduct a body search of each and every inmate. From this point onwards, everything was done with excess aggression. One by one we were boldly groped as they felt for any contraband. This show was just as much to restore order as it was to realign their manhood. Moments ago these same overly brash officers stood by, tails tucked and frightened, as a man they were meant to protect was brutally assaulted; much enthused now to assert themselves. The belief of every life being worth its weight in gold was turned on and off with convenience. The same refused to acknowledge that a prison sentence married inside and outside worlds. Prison did not aid, it ailed, but this they already knew.

Entering my unit was like walking into a mad house. Again C.O's were yelling, *"Lockdown!"* Inmates scrambled back and forth from the phone, ice machine, showers, and cells, attempting to secure any food that could hold one over (peanut butter, jelly and soups). Certain groups huddled up discussing what had transpired. Revenge was definite. No group attacked another without retaliation. Each group had to maintain their prison status. Allowing someone from another geographical location, gang, or group to take out one of yours was a no-go!

****

Locked back inside the stinginess of my double bunked cell, I was left to mentally survey the *'unseen'* events that were linked together. Somewhere in America a white man's justice was becoming another black man's grief as a prosecutor rants, and a judge callously abides by sentencing yet another to forever. Anything close to compassion was mangled. This mangling of conscience contributes to the loss of one's bearings and emotional destruction. Hardened by a system so cold, one becomes capable of killing with a smile. The same childhood smile which graced the photos above his living room mantelpiece. His family with images of their baby: the system with a mug shot of a murderer.

The slain man's family phone will ring interrupting their daily lives. The caller I.D. will read *'unknown'*, the phone will be answered with the sweetest of hellos and on the other line, the prison Chaplain will speak with a soft whisper,

"Mr. and Mrs. I'm afraid your son has been declared deceased."

Nothing further; no excuse, no reason, and no compassion. The blood was on the hands of not only the accused, but that of the criminal justice system, which refused to acknowledge that prison did more than reform. The long list of detriments far exceeded the negative behavioral deterrents.

"Get out of that daze. They're opening the doors," my cellie informed.

"They're opening the doors?" I asked, surprised that after the events from earlier they would allow us to function so soon.

"Yeah, they're opening the doors. This type of shit happens on the regular. Why would they keep us on lockdown when us killing one another is part of their plan?"

A cold world traded in for an even colder system.

"Crazy!" I mumbled so only I could hear. I was in an absolute state of disbelief. Maybe this was their plan. Of course I didn't want to be locked down, so questioning it any further was out of the question. However, there were some things that screamed, *"This can't be right!"* This was one of them.

To my surprise, it was only a few short hours which passed before the racket of the penitentiary resumed. One after another, men began exiting their cells unable to contain the latest gossip.

"Did you see how he hit the dude?"

"Where was dude from?"

"I wonder if the dude gonna make it?"

That was the extent of the concern. Emotionless, while starving to be understood. Many don't know what it means to feel. We're taught when entering these doors that emotions can only get in the way of what it takes to survive. Emotional callousness becomes a safeguard from the possibility of becoming prey.

For the second time around Main Line was called. The already fast pace of the prison was moving even faster; zero to a hundred. A second wave of violence was anticipated by all. Up and down the corridor there stood a heavy officer presence with panic buttons ready to be hit, mace primed, and cuffs clicking. The hall was disturbingly quiet. There was to be no mistake. The momentary calm did not rule out the impending storm.

I finally made it to the Chow Hall. Once inside, the ruckus immediately reminded me of a high school cafeteria, minus the exuberant demeanor of children without a worry in the world. From what I could see, there were rows of tables, front to back, side to side, beverage machines, and a salad bar. The inmate kitchen workers were shaking spoons of chow, serving minimal portions of slop. Officers stood over their shoulders threatening to fire anyone who slid a third slice of bread. To them, three hot meals were too much for criminals.

While there was too little food being served, inmate kitchen workers made due by stealing the leftover food and reselling the meals. Five postage stamps for a sandwich and twenty mailing stamps for a styrofoam tray. We had to eat somehow. Little did we in the general population know that the majority of this food was ours anyway. It was either stolen or, more or less, recovered from the back docks trash bin.

Inmates hurried through the line, scanning their I.D's like credit cards at the local shopping mall. More staff in Brooks Brother's suits, and flat bottomed Steve Madden shoes, stood in the middle of the Chow Hall clearly displeased by the look written all over their faces.

To be in the immediate presence of inmates irked their nerves. It was as if they hadn't applied to be a servant to us. Inmates bum-rushed the staff with grievances and concerns. This only agitated the staff even more. To sit and rot was their expectation. Fighting for our freedom was beyond their realm of reality. Egregious conditions were to be silently accepted.

In addition, there were few smiles, smirks, gritted expressions and solemn stares. Ironically, all was alive. Briefly, hostility was replaced by hunger. My cellie, a younger kid from Brooklyn, New York, pointed out to me the '*only*' tables I was allowed to sit and eat. The Chow Hall, by our own doing, had been divided just as the prison population. Whites sat here, blacks sat there. Bloods, Crips, cities, and states all had their own allotted areas to eat. There was even division amongst religious groups (Christians, Nation of Islam, Sunni Muslims, and the Moor Science Temple of America).

With my own eyes I was seeing the worlds all embracing religious groups succumbing to segregation. Prison politics was prompting religious innovation. The devil's hand was surely at work. I worried if the evils of the penitentiary were more powerful than the practices of peace. Little be known, the administration enjoyed every element of this separation. Away from our differences stood at least one common denominator; freedom. Nevertheless, we seemed unable to remove our blinders.

You couldn't cut between the tables in the Chow Hall. You couldn't sit in an area where you were not from or with a group you did not '*run*' with. Men tapped the tables twice with their knuckles as they departed as a show of respect, and cutting the line would end badly. These were small things which could easily turn major if overlooked.

Not soon after my '*5-star meal*' it was straight to the Rec Yard. One large space divided into four smaller yards. Amid the four sub yards there was a handball, basketball, and a bocce ball court. There was also was a horseshoe ring, baseball and football field, a circular track, and a few metal bleachers. More importantly, was the fence topped with barbed wire and the correction officers toting assault rifles manning gun towers.

The Rec Yard reminded me of the Oval Park in which I was raised. It was a coliseum fit for gladiators. With absolute disregard for authority, many men took to the prison Rec Yard to put down the most violent acts one could imagine. Initially, I couldn't figure this out as there was absolutely no chance of escape. However, plans of retreat were not in the cards. The yard set the biggest stage and a violent performance could echo from prison to prison. Life in prison was more show and less tell. If you couldn't demonstrate that you were ready, willing, and able, despite the emptiness of the act, your days were numbered. Months later I would be on this same stage (Rec Yard), in a ten-man brawl, only several feet beneath the gun tower, until officers rushed in demanding all inmates to *"Get On The Ground NOW!"*

****

On the Rec Yard, prisoners moved about hustling provocative pictures, self made candy, shoes, even altered clothing. The yard fluctuated from rec, round table, flea market, brewery, and the battlefield. Through the hustle and bustle, I met with my remaining homies and the one man who was said to be the yards *'shot caller'*. A shot caller was the general. He was the one who ultimately made the decisions for specified groups and gangs. His decision was often the call which decided peace or war. Apart from prison's spontaneous acts of brutality, much of its force was the result of a *'shot'* being called. Continuing around the track, every few short paces or so there was a subtle head nod indicating the presence of another gang, group or state affiliate. *"Yeah, new beginnings,"* I thought.

After the initial greetings of, *"What's poppin'? What spot you came from? How much time you got?"* we began walking the track. Side by side, the shot caller and I spun the track with three homies trailing. Homies who would remain so, unless a 'shot' was called saying otherwise. I took this as all being routine. Everywhere I looked I saw those whom I had arrived with being taken through the same dramatics. However, this was no act. No one lost sight of what bus day represented. New faces symbolized a threat. Prison yards were figuratively run by prisoners. Seniority at a prison gave many the false and foolish impression that the longer their stay, the more rights they had over the prison. These new faces, our news faces, and my new face, was a liability.

Out of a bus of twenty plus arrivals, an estimated third wouldn't make it past the first 48 hours. Nearly the entire population had eaten, and rushed to the yard, all eyes and ears. Like thieves in the heat of the night, men stood with legs crossed, leaning against the gates, and with arms folded. One hand was covering their mouth as they scanned the premises with predatory scowls. If there were any lingering disputes, skeletons, or simply predators on a prowl for prey, it wouldn't be long. You couldn't let a potential threat persist and for that reason alone bus days were most intense.

With penitentiaries spread all across America, one would assume that word travels at a snail's pace or hiding out would come with little difficulty. However, the word on who was who, and what was what, often arrived before an inmate did. Tracking down names and registration numbers was elementary to those who desired such information. Envision a prisoner, worn down, mind and body; fatigued from hours, days, and weeks of traveling from one side of the globe to the next; weighed down by leg irons, metal linked waist chains fastened tight, and silver handcuffs. Your only meal was bologna and cheese for all three meals; purposely making you famished. He exits the bus, slowly hopping his way into the prison, aware of the potential danger but oblivious to earlier developments.

Prior to his arrival there was a kite (letter). The weight of this kite was enormous. It was a hit! Somewhere on the prison yard stood men with no face, prepared to make their presence felt. There were no care packages, only full out aggression and prison-made shanks. The only delay of one attack was another attack. Just around the corner from a bus arrival were body alarms sounding in succession.

Prison was run by brute force. Penitentiary violence forces you to confront the reality of just how slim your chances were of making it home. The baddest mothafuckas wear thin and were ripped to shreds. Around the clock there were deliberate killings, even accidental murders. The machete styled sharpened pieces of steel were for more than show. They were meant to send men to meet their makers before another man permanently put you on chill.

Yes, freedom and family stay at the front of every man's mind, even those who can't see the forest for all the trees. However, making it home was no guarantee. It all came down to doing what you had to do with hopes you didn't '*get got*' in the process. The preference was to be judged by twelve before being carried by six. Men have lost their lives tiptoeing around prison, fixated by the notion one could actually '*duck*' the endless stream of violence which rages through the system like Hurricane Sandy.

Misery and violence were prevalent. Men slit their own wrists, hung themselves, intentionally overdose, and some even attempt death by cop. Coming face to face with the ever present violence of prison was inevitable. The stories of rapes, the brutal beatings with locks in socks, the strong armed robberies where men stick their hands in the asses of other men, take their drugs, smoke them in their face, pat them on the back and flee the scene in hot pursuit of their next victim were real. In part, these acts of violence weren't personal (direct disrespect). It stems from pinned up frustration, anger, and disappointment in self, wrongly released on one's peers.

Others would argue the savagery was but a means of surviving, thus the violence draws a symbolism to that of needing water to live. The violence makes men feel '*alive*'. The exertion of power, of the force over another human after being abused and battered by a system, was intoxicating. You drink it up and if your hands weren't gripping the shanks, concussing men with locks in socks, or spreading the asses of men like the very people you despise (correction officers), your mind comes to know the violence on a first name basis. So much so that two men going toe to toe, trading blows like Ali and Foreman (rumble in the jungle), were considered faking; not really wanting any work.

Having survived the overkill of arresting officers, County Jail trustees, US Marshals, and BOP staff, there lives an expectation of anger, to be mad, and violent. And who else did our underdeveloped minds construe as the enemy – our self! From afar witnessing this degree of violence rationalized critics negative positions towards violent offenders. However, for argument's sake, allow me to educate you.

* Christopher Columbus and his companions violently took this land from Native Americans.

* America and its upstanding citizens turned their heads for over 400 years as African Americans were violently assaulted.

* After 400 years of violence, America finally gives an inch with voting bills and civil rights, yet as a result we were violently beaten some more.

* Turn on your television and what do you see? Trayvon, Eric, Phillando, and Tamir. All victims of excessive force and violence by law enforcement.

* Our beloved president of the United States has been elected only after truth spilled of him abusing women because, in his own words, '*money makes it okay*'.

Violence begets violence people!

Shine the light on any of my words, "I am not an advocate of violence". Thus it was impossible to wage war on the rights of man without the expectancy of rebellion.

****

July 19th, 2019 the federal government passed a prison reform bill, '*First Step Act*'. This particular bill positively impacts federal prisoners with the exception of violent offenders.

Once again, America chops off its nose to spite its face.

Continuing around the track, every few short paces or so there was a subtle headnod indicating the presence of another gang, group, or state affiliate. Whispers of, "See him right there to the left? That's the Shot Caller. When it goes down, that's who we want to hit." Premeditating a hit within the first 24 hours on the yard was a clear indication of what lay ahead. '*Yeah, new beginnings,*' I thought.

From the initial sizing, every measurable extent of prison life appeared violent. Was this all there was to it? Were there not men who desired freedom, justice, equality, peace, and truth? Contrary to what prison advocates and shareholders want you to believe, there were those who had high morals and who honored principles. There were also those who spent every waking minute with their heads buried inside law books, bibles, and Qurans. There were even those who believed they themselves were GOD. These were the men who preferred to seal their casket closed before harming another individual or disrupting the progression of another.

This was the truth that was intentionally hidden. For it was in their vested interest to promote violence, and to shield you from the fact that prison produces the very thing it was said to cure. Note, as defined by law, a violent crime does not necessarily constitute bodily harm, intentional, or unintentional. In 2019 thousands of violent crime convictions were overturned as a result of the vague definition regarding a crime of violence (United States vs. Johnson Circuit, United States vs. Davis Circuit).

The numbers can be misleading. Educated by experience, over time, I learned that alot of violence committed in prison against others was to prevent violence against one's self. Basically, behavior was shaped by the environment such as the ghetto, jungle, and the penitentiary. Consistent among them all was the predator to prey and the desperation to survival disposition.

The occupants of these territories would do anything to survive, even if that means preying on one another. Oppression, miseducation, and poverty places survival ahead of reasoning. A hardened life overshadowed '*I have a dream*' speeches. A starving man will eat his own flesh, if it means survival. Was this act one of savagery, barbarism, or plain logic for one who wants to live? The truth was not a justification, its nothing more and nothing less than the truth.

With each lap I was further enlightened on the prison inmate imposed rules and regulations. It was a convicts code of conduct. Stressed heavily was this unwritten record that decided life and death. Sadly, the injustices being served on us all by the system were not included on this list. This list proved our continued lack of understanding, and showed how we missed the fact that we were being oppressed, manipulated, and exploited. While we used masculinity to justify what we unjustly did to ourselves, the real culprits sat back smiling and enjoying the show. We were demanding to be unchained, but at the same time binding ourselves.

This verbal list of prisoner-imposed rules contained the likes of where you could sit and which televisions you could watch. It stated that there would be no running up debts of any kind; who was protected by way of "hands off" policies; who you were allowed to cell with; and how many days you had to present legal documentation. Who had concocted this Molotov cocktail of limitations? One would never know. If I had to put my money on it for a sure shot, it would be the same individuals who erected the walls that keep us at bay.

In spite of my dislike of these self-imposed regulations, they shaped an otherwise orderless environment. Prison could be chaotic around the clock, and often was. With no '*rules*' amongst us prisoners, things were bound to explode. Therefore, while this list of rules kept the respect level high among prisoners, the admiration and appreciation were a result of fear. You violate the rules and you knew someone was on their way to put you back in line. This self-proclaimed respect heightened distrust and made distance best. Approachable, but not sociable. Powerful minds weakened through separation. A small part of their plan was beginning to reveal itself.

As I followed the last few laps around the track, "yard recall" was sounded. Hordes of men that were gathered in groups shook hands and made last second trades. The homies and I sent farewells, sure that we would be seeing one another sooner than later. In prison, the space was minimal and the actions repetitive.

The remainder of the day moved in a blur. Each of my co-defendants chaperoned me from the laundry to the commissary, then back to the unit. At the laundry, I was provided with *'free'* prison garbs (three beige pants, three beige shirts, three boxer shorts, t-shirts and socks). This issuing of clothing, all the way down to the socks, was paid for with something far greater than riches. It was paid with our lives, our time, and our freedom.

Nothing was free in the prison commissary. Items were grossly overpriced and ridiculously understocked (4$ soap, 5$ toothpaste, 6$ shampoo). Yet, we were granted, in some cases, a monthly salary as scant as $5.25. A decent shower could run you three months of hard labor. Sure, there were generic items for far less, and prison-issued toiletries which left you with blotchy skin and did little to eliminate the stench of prison. Could this continued creation of deprivation and desperation enhance prison violence? Quite possible. Had this atrocity been anywhere on the other side of this wall, the world would be screaming "exploitation", but since we were sentenced criminals, no one cried foul.

Later on into the night, after the doors were locked and my cellie had drifted off to sleep, I lay atop my bunk, arms behind my head, fingers locked, staring at the ceiling. There was much to process. All to be valued with the weight of a ten ton wrecking ball. I was now free to walk a straight line. The straight-line I must admit was a lane I had evaded. Yet the right of way required that I be rare: rare, accountable, respectful, and earnest. Finding my way would be the true test.

****

Day 1…Day 2…Day 3…Day 4…

I keep moving. Each day mirrors the last with no one boasting about tomorrow. No one knew what the day would bring. Without even a third of my stint in, I definitely didn't want to get into the habit of counting days since I wanted to maintain my sanity. From January to December I was doing time. Time that resembled sand in an hourglass kept elapsing slowly into more time.

Time was worn like a badge of honor, and too much time had the same *'gangsta'* bawling uncontrollably. In time the grays set in, hairlines begin to fade and one's mental state starts to slip. Was there really a thing as too little time?

So what was this time? Time to punish, time to bend, time to break! However, if I wanted to survive my first thirty days, I needed to keep track. Thirty days were a convict's window to provide legal documentation. We call it *'paperwork'.* A prisoner's American express; *Don't leave home without it.*

This paperwork provided proof that you took your hit like a man. There was nothing which carried greater significance in the penitentiary. True, a pair a lips would say anything, therefore black and white legal documentation minimized the gibberish and spoke the loudest. It stated what you were arrested for, sentenced to, and whether or not you had shifted the burden of responsibility and punishment to another. Your favorite rappers often rap about *'paperwork'.* Many take its weight with a grain of salt, figuring it to be only rap lyrics. On the inside, to be about that life, you were demanded to prove that you lived that life.

Nearly 3/4's of men and women inside prison, federal or state, were locked away as a consequence of someone assisting law enforcement. If you asked a man in prison, "What do you despise the most?" the answer would be, "A rat!" This was the lowest form of treachery within the underworld. This degree of betrayal was rooted against from the soiled streets of New Jersey to the Nations Capital.

My apologies for breaking the news, but were we to believe that our law enforcement agencies were simply top shelf Matlock types who run out, leave behind their doughnuts and coffee, and tackle criminals red handed with their hands buried deep inside the cookie jar? What we have were overly aggressive, bully tactic applicants, citizen abusers, and taxpayer money wasters. Most have threatened, coerced, and manipulated situations, statements, and evidence to support their claim and award them with more time to finger Krispy Kremes, and Mocholattes. After they have eased their work, they take these same '*cooperators*' and throw them to the wolves, yes, inside the same hellfire pit where they have condemned others to eternal darkness. Two birds with one stone.

I'm certain conservative minds view this theory in terms of smooth criminals desire to indulge in a life of crime; while citizens of 'an equal opportunity America' remain silent. This was not true. Those of us on the inside view betrayal through the same lenses in which you envision treason committed against America.

"The code of the streets was the code of the world." -Ta-Nehisi Coates.

See the violation of allegiance with respect to friendship the same as you do the American flag. Furthermore, picture the betrayal of our Criminal Justice System which proclaims to be colorblind and ethically balanced, yet pardons shameful acts of one merely to prosecute another.

One of the most memorable displays of how 'profitable' crime was and how unjust our system is, was in the 1990's when the Criminal Justice System discounted multiple murders committed by one, Sammy the Bull. A hitman for the then Italian mob, run by John Gotti. The Bull candidly admitted to killing in cold blood on the behest of John Gotti. Our government and its thirst for headlines awarded the Bull immunity only for him to later run into law enforcement, accused of running a drug ring. What did the acceptance of this behavior tell society? We were accepting of crime for as long as it assists in America's grand scheme. What was this grand scheme? Mass incarceration.

Note: aiding in law enforcement does not remove one from negative categorizing applied to those involved in a life of crime, even if said crime was minimal. Be sure to read the fine print, "While your testimony may shorten your prison term, this term will award the most difficult time of your life."

Around twenty days or so days had passes; 4 o'clock count had been cleared. The unit doors were opened. In its prescribed order, men gathered around the units horseshoe desk preparing for the unit officer to announce, '*mail call*'. Five days a week men relived this moment, for indeed it was a '*moment*'. Paper touched by ink, wrapped in a 4x9 inch envelope. Hopefully, sealed with a kiss. No matter where the mail arrived from, or who was the sender, there need not be a sealed kiss. Though, the thought alone was a gift of life. For at least one minute of someone's day, life stopped and you took precedence: not work, not bills, not Sunday night sitcoms, but you. Damn, what a feeling! To be remembered was to be alive. To be forgotten was emotional and psychological torture.

Shoulder to shoulder, everyone was quiet, secretly praying, '*Just one letter*'. An old love, mother, brother, or sister; any news was good news. Unfortunately, the rapid pace of the free world: advanced technology, instant messaging, social media, frivolous consumption ($400 cell phones), and stone hearts (that's the life he chose, now he must deal with it), has left many forgotten. Not all in this anxiety-riddled huddle would walk away feeling high spirited. As the mail pile dwindled, you could hear the low sighs and read the frustration on their faces. Some have waited years for that '*one letter*'.

"Butler 050," shouted the C.O. "It's your lucky day," he said while handing me a large manila envelope.

Having been around long enough, the C.O. knew exactly what the envelope held inside. "That's it, fellas. You weren't running around behind your family in those streets, so don't be running up here for mail now."

The truthfulness of his joke stung, for most knew while on the outside, family had been looked over as we chased the nothingness of the streets.

"Fuck you!" a prisoner returned speaking more from hurt than anger.

I had applied to the school of hard knocks. In my hands, I held my acceptance papers. My federal attorney Wanda Akin had forwarded a copy of my plea agreement, transcripts, and sentence submissions. Enough of the insignificant chatter, it was time to produce. Though it may not have been verbally spoken, I knew all were counting the days as was I. In prison, no one wanted to associate with the island's cast off. With paperwork in tow, I held the answers to all questions. Doing as I was told, I handed over my paperwork to the prisons Shot Caller. Seventy-Two hours later, my paperwork had been cleared. I was given my knife and my bid began.

****

The beginning of winter was fast approaching. The chill of prison life was in a race with December's frigidness. For most, the Rec Yard was given up for the prison gymnasium. I thoroughly enjoyed this time of year. The overcrowded space made ease virtually impossible. A single hour alone on the Rec Yard awarded the tranquility of a thousand '*woosahs*'.

Myself and a few others would walk the track bundled up in our prison issued jackets, knitted caps, and firm grips on mugs full of jet black coffee. The small number of prisoners who chose to bear the cold, in all likelihood, were in pursuit of a small piece of peace. Prison didn't award calm, and neither had the downtrodden neighborhoods which led us here. The short-lived sereneness of the unattended Rec Yard reminded me of my childhood before realizing a young black man in America was a target. Even at a young age, one understood what it felt like to be targeted (stopped and frisked).

Unmarked police cars packed to the brim, eyes like infrared beams, doors ajar, ready to profile and pounce, their duties confused; protect and serve, harass and assault. Unafraid and unapologetically, we gave the middle finger to crooked cops. This fearlessness further enhanced the targets on our backs.

For decades poor communities have been stigmatized as being full of flagrants to excuse racial profiling and mass incarceration. They were commissioned by commanding figureheads to check the temperature of the poor. Despite resistance being a natural reaction, defiance spawned disguised attacks in communities where minorities were the majority. In the middle of the night raids, women and kids cuffed like criminals, some shot down in cold blood, heartlessly murdered. think Breonna Taylor, Amadou Diallo, Sean bell, Michael Brown, Eric Garner, now George Floyd.

The ghetto was a war zone and here I stood trying to steal a moment's peace on a prison yard. Although the Rec Yard was quiet, my immediate surroundings were a reminder that peace may very well remain just outside of arm's reach. I walked around in circles wishing that the track would somehow open up and permit me to venture into parts of the world unknown; that one day I would be able to shed the shackles, to touch the four corners of the earth. So wonderful it was to dream.

In an instant, the yard was recalled and the unpleasant experiences, which went along with this nightmarish existence, took to the forefront. At every turn, scattered across the compound, were those who had fought tooth and nail to maintain their sanity, the strong-willed, the conscious. On the flip side, in droves resembling a Stephen King horror flick, men were moving like zombies, drugged till unresponsive. The mentally ill were in a place they did not belong: prison.

The criminal justice system professed prison as a fix all. Undoubtedly, men and women belonging under the care of professional help, instead, were force-fed psychiatric medications in doses powerful enough to put down a raging bull. They were mutated into mummies as a result of mental paralysis. Experimental drugs had been pushed into their bloodstreams; their sanity was now a distant stranger.

Evaluated and diagnosed, the same treatment went to everyone *'criminal'*, controlled only through the force of the system's iron fist. Their mental instabilities were abused. Prisoners could be seen speaking to themselves while their demons spoke back to them. They were in deep nods, rocking back and forth, unable to participate in a conversation. How does prison assist a man who is too doped up to simply utter his name?

The mental deterioration one undergoes inside of these walls was ever dangerous. More so that many do not recognize their fading health until it was often too late. At this time the subtle parodies provoked by the puppeteer had taken shape slowly, but surely. The mental assaults and deadly mind-games played by the administration creeps up like a lion stalking its prey. Dignity wanes as men cheer when fried chicken was served for lunch; or one sprints from their cell the instant the door was opened, rushing to catch *'Maury'* in the morning.

They were unashamed by their lack of personal hygiene as long as their cell floor was spit shined to perfection. No rhyme, no reason. Lulled to sleep by a system which in itself was crazed. The lack of consciousness and self worth, partnered with the psychological torturing, left a great portion of the prison population walking accidents. This wasn't the place where God looked out for fools and babies. Not only do you have to think for yourself, you have to think for them as well. A short circuit in your psyche could get you tuned up. Prisoners aren't doctors and can't differentiate crazy from ka-ray-zee. Oftentimes, you'll discover someone with real mental issues sprawled out on the yard with six inches of steel pressed deep into their gut. Those of us with enough common sense would question if this was administrations way of covertly keeping the pot stirred.

This was prison's cruel creation of an unbreakable cycle of dependency. You can attempt to draw a difference between crack addicts in the ghetto, and the psyche medication-addicted inmate who becomes gravely dependent on the *'drug'*. Staring out of your cell window, you could see the prisons pill line stretching the length of the entire compound; sights of men scratching holes the size of quarters into their flesh, nervous systems shot, unable to stand still.

The prison was peddling medication like dope boys pushing crack cocaine out of dope houses. The intangible, yet real benefit of this process was control. It was the process of owning a man through medication. To them, reform was verbiage for robbing man of his truest self, dominating his person in full until he was no more the same. Prison restricted the physical anatomy; thus, prison operated under this pretense - in order to dominate, the trapping of the mind had to be enforced.

Psychiatric medications implemented erroneously demonstrated the correction of certain behaviors (fights, outbursts). These actions were actually commonplace in a hostile environment. As year after year, another legalized basis for removing leisure activity for inmates was discovered, minimizing the time spent outside of the cell. Another fictitious reasoning would be introduced to sedate inmate after inmate. On the other hand, medication wasn't the only thing happening that had inmates *'stuck'*.

In years passed, I have been placed in numerous cells containing men with mental disorders. The administration preferred I rid them of the *'headache'* by beating them senseless; truly testing my will and to see if I had actually changed. I would be up all night attempting to talk them off the ledge, while struggling with myself not to personalize their illness. On occasion I would tremble with anger, nose sweating, fist balled, and ready to strike. Buried beneath my blanket, I was furious at the games people played and the obvious obsequiousness by a fellow convict.

In war there were casualties and these were the lost soldiers. Though we dared not leave any behind, once one's mind took flight, the body became a vegetable rotting in muddy waters. A somber sight was the destruction of men who were once ever prideful. They were transformed into mental patients, savages, sexual predators, homosexuals, synthetic drug addicts, and pure dope users. Without so much as laying a finger on you (although they didn't hesitate to beat you to a pulp), the system stripped you of your identity.

I began rehashing the innumerable stories told by inmates in their attempts to save face. Stories of the four-car garage lined with a Rolls Royce, Beamer, Bentley, and a Benz. The fleet of women from Brooklyn to Brazil and an insurmountable amount of wealth. Yet, right now these same men didn't have a pennies worth of dignity left when "time" began biting like a pit bull off its leash. Now they won't even wash their ass.

****

Such debilitating tactics were applied, but never uttered. On the outside, the government had dismissed our children (canceling Head Start), forgotten our elderly (terminating Obamacare), gave war veterans suffering from PTSD no love, and we, the imprisoned, were being killed. We were being terminated by way of psychological warfare. This was how many were broken. This system aimed to cripple anything that resembled strength; to assassinate the little bit of decency man had, from stripping you and forcing you to bend at the waist, to beating you till you cried for mercy. This happened anytime a man decided to fight back.

Much of this damage was irreversible and beyond medicinal repair. These mental games were killing minds and spirit to the point of nothing ever being okay again. These games would make men stop calling home, forget about their freedom, trade off their property, and, if possible, sell their souls to the highest bidder. They were made weak by a system that gathered its ammunition from your hard-earned tax dollars. Countless prisoners were being toppled due to societies silence, not only in the back of a man's mind, but the center of his prefrontal cortex was the plight of the imprisoned and the pain of seemingly being forgotten. #justicefortheincarcerated

In what ways do we define justice? To date, my trials had not led me to the use of medication. My prison sentence of thirty years had not made me into a mummy. However, my connection to those I struggled alongside caused me to feel the pain of those who were being mummified. Similar to the emotional properties I held as a child, I hated to witness those close to me suffer. In prison there were invisible scars whipped onto the minds and souls of my peers. Every day was a day of darkness and light seemed forever distant.

We were all fighting the same cruelty. The system's motif was to pound away at our sanity with a sledge hammer called justice. This was not a one on one battle, but a collective bludgeoning of us all. The string of assaults had a pitiless effect on prisoners. Each action on behalf of the criminal justice system was a billboard advising people to remain frightened. Attempts at scaring people down the right path was of little benefit, but when dealing with the reality of it all, you understand it was too grave to get caught dreaming, yet many were.

To keep awake, most days, I would find ways to separate myself from everything and everyone. I had a deep desire to be alone. The incessant random behaviors of the population were blocking my composure. My personality became borderline repulsive. In my interactions, from my phone calls home to the letters I forwarded, I couldn't deliver a warm greeting. My mouth couldn't move to ask, *'How are you doing?'* My hands couldn't remember the motion to write, *'I love you!'*

I'm certain that during this period, the few family and friends I had left found me difficult to deal with. The emotional transfiguration was incomprehensible. While they didn't understand, my belief had become that in order for me to hang on, I needed to rebel against the eventual farewell friend. I was beginning to change, but not in the fashion I desired.

I couldn't remove the sight of men with no more life in their lungs, and a bed sheet tightly wrapped around their necks from my mind. They were unable to keep control under the climate of unexpected goodbyes and I couldn't allow this to be me. I'd begun to lash out, even at those whom my heart believed were sincere and I discovered complications when attempting to reciprocate emotionally.

Prison was demanding. I recalled loved ones questioning my altered state.

"What's the matter?"

"Are you okay?"

I was growing more silent and unsure of how to answer. There were no words to describe or define what I was feeling. Some things were impossible to fathom, barring the experience itself. Too many years had passed and too many years were left to come.

The many layers of confinement were finely crafted. Fading friends and their broken promises became equally as oppressive as the system; a system that did everything in its power to shatter a man's means of companionship. Though I refused to count the days until freedom, I couldn't resist counting the days leading to when another friend would stop answering the phone; or when another female fell in love with the feel of a sexual encounter, and stopped believing that true love held the perfect recipe to defeat the distance and time brought on by confinement.

Detachment, physical and emotional seclusion were definitely the best options. My talks about modern-day slavery, Jim Crow laws, and criminal injustice, didn't stand a chance against the latest fashion trends or integral and recent twitter disputes. There was nothing soft when I spoke, yet to hear me seemed problematic. My struggle in no way compared to Janet Jackson's concerts, Kim K's breaking the internet, or basking in the sun on Dubai's white sands. Matters involving prisoner abuse, prison reform or simply an imprisoned loved one dying from lack of companionship, were not as alluring. The revolution was being televised.

****

Overwhelmed and irate, the doorway of my darkened cell became my retreat. Of course I still listened and watched, but mostly I sat staring at the clock, contemplating the end: a time when the numbers could no longer taunt me and I could no longer run from the truth. The obvious had to be accepted, then confronted, regardless of the associated affliction. There was no greater pain than that brought on by puppet politicians trying to fix what was intentionally broken.

Badgering and beating in my brain like a bass drum was that damn clock. With my eyes closed and both hands pressed against my ears, I attempted to drown out the clock's deliberate harassment. Each passing minute, another family was being torn apart and another prison being built. Do we need additional evidence to show how prison confines a family? It was lineal destruction. Generation after generation, with our grandbabies awaiting prison sentences. That was what they promised us for tomorrow.

In a hurry, I learned to keep my distance from this clock. It read that the time was now because not everyone would be blessed with another day. Continuously putting off what could no longer be put off was self-destructive and procrastination was but movement in the wrong direction. The scant possibility of surviving to see another twenty-four hours made it impossible to think ahead. This clock taught me the vast nature of impulsive men in prison. Instant action was not so much a desire to act without reflection, but a need not for stuttering steps. Incarcerated men could not be stationed. In a writing to Angela Davis, revolutionary general George Jackson quoted comrade Che Guevara as follows: "One does not wait for the conditions to be right. To start the revolution, the forces of the revolution itself will make the conditions to be right."

Please understand that not all revolutions were a call to violence. Yet through the study of self, and through learning the history of the primordial man, I grew to appreciate the propensity of imprisoned people to move. A delayed response in breaking the chains, which had choked men and women since America's birth, was more costly than many let on. We, as shackled souls, were the expense.

Perhaps my sprouting passion of opposing further procrastination was written on my face. As I sat assessing my surroundings from my cell door, having never spoken, I was approached by a dark skinned veteran convict. He had a slight stocky build and was from the city of Baltimore. From what I knew, this man was one of few words. Handing me a folded piece of paper was a quote from OG Mandino's University of Success.

"The difference between wise men and fools is often found in their choice of tools."

"Aye, Black," I called across the tier. As if stunned that I knew his name, he spun around with furrowed brows.

"What's up, yo?"

"What's this all about?" I asked, holding up the piece of paper.

"You'll figure it out," said Black, ending the conversation just as quickly as it started before moving on.

Figure it out was exactly what I would do and when I did, I had every intention of making Black aware. Surely this was a test and I was never one to not show up when called upon. I was twenty-eight years of age at this point and no spring chicken. Neither could I be considered a seasoned vet. Surely Black, along with others, had watched, week after week, bus load after bus load, young kids barely legal, enter the penitentiary with sentences twice that of the voter registration eligibility. For whatever reason, he had taken an interest in me and let on that he could see my potential.

These young men were as clueless as I when I first arrived in the system. Every muscle was used to putting food on the table; an action that proved to be more physical than mental. Their lack of education continually played them right into the hands of this perilous system. Undoubtedly the summation of Black's message was, *'A wise man was an organized man. A self-controlled man. A disciplined one who understood that man's greatest tool is that of his mind and not his body.'*

The verbiage, *'mind over matter,'* was meaningful in reaching one's goals. Experience was indeed the best teacher. Without the intellect to rightly interpret the experience, our comprehension can work either for or against victory. Regardless, the arena was secured through education and organization. When to act and how to act was easily debatable. What could never be disclaimed was the necessity of the masses in knowing what they were fighting for and who they were fighting against.

Educate, organize, and fight!

My chameleon persona that was adapting readily to my surrounding circumstances had vanished. This was not a reality to grow accustomed to. The system's abnormal approach at correction was more complex than imagined. Particularly, our fight was directed at the imbalance of justice, not prison reform or mandatory minimums, but at societal change: fighting against the injustices that we not only suffered on the inside, but the injustices which played an intricate role in us being imprisoned. Our fight was to free each other one at a time. This awarded us a trusted comrade who knew the hardships, endured the suffering and understood that spilling the truth on the outside freed those of us left behind. It was symbolic of building a great pyramid, one brick at a time.

Unfortunately prison was no playground. Few fraternized, so organizing was a near-impossible feat. The administration wouldn't dare allow the prison population to unite. Lockdown, transfers, and even physical abuse would be enforced as a result. In addition, we moved as though blindfolds were permanently fastened over our eyelids. The identity of a bold-faced enemy went unnoticed. Too many men were busy pretending to be 6'7", 280lbs for the sake of appearing unapproachable.

The concept of U.N.I.T.Y was being lost in vanity, and freedom was being washed away in the bloodshed of prison politics. Slicing at the jugular of the prison population was ignorance, individualism, and arrogance. The conniving characteristics of a misguided comrades creed made intentions hard to decipher.

As cells were being converted into classrooms, the viewpoint of war strategists was placed on the plates of prisoners to eat up. Misappropriated philosophies were harming the cause and meticulously scripted stratagems were being aimed at one another. Knowledge was by all means power. While a simpleton was sure to be drunk on misunderstanding, the hope of freedom fighters was constantly at odds with deception. Backward imitators imagining themselves to be penitentiary Genghis Khans and Sun Tzu's. These existed as an array of hurdles in forging bonds behind the wall. The honoring of principles that discounted humanity stunted the process of building unburnable bridges and faulty interpretations of what a man was and what a man should be.

Except for the inmates who wore extra tight clothing, switched their hips like women when they walked, and used Kool-Aid packs for lipstick, everyone deemed themselves a man. Irony aside, a man defined in prison held many meanings. They strived to be the most aggressive, show blatant homophobia, and stack plenty of money. Regardless of the different ideas of what made a man, a man's worth was weighed by his ability to stand up despite how far he fell. When it came to believing in our ability to overcome, it was essential that I remained steadfast.

At 5 a.m. every morning, amid corrupting thoughts, the cells were still locked and rooms absent of light. You could hear the screeching sounds of metal being scraped against the cement floors. Men with gloved hands to shield the heat were readying for war. The noise would rise from cell to cell. There were no warped images of what was being done. By 5:45 a.m. the prisoners were fully dressed, standing at their doors like racehorses at the opening gate. Who would rush who? Who would play the sly fox and angle their man into a corner when the time was right? Men were made several pounds heavier from hardcover books wrapped around their abdominals and chest plates.

Revolutionary Suicide on a Prison Yard. Boom!

****

I can't recall a single night since I'd been locked up where I actually slept. I was always forced to keep one eye open while resting, but well prepared. I wasn't afraid, I was alert. The best got served and individuals closest to you woke you out of your sleep. All you'd see were smiling faces while you were groggy and clueless. Then there came endless death blows pressing you closer to the grave. There would be stabbing at your flesh, blood painting the walls, and a pool of blood on the floor. It was the darkest truth of them all.

A prisons' blues held no poetic rhythm. For those who pushed against the current of prison were not synchronized. Here there always lived confusion where chaos was forever repeated. If we wanted to succeed, we had to find commonality in cause and move!

Chapter 3
Involuntary Servitude

The unit held one hundred and twenty eight prisoners within sixty four cells, and ran two stories high.. Additionally, there were eight showers, two activity rooms, iron table tops, and six television sets that were racially divided. The televisions were always on sports, music videos or the movie of the week (Nikki Minaj overran CNN). Not many dared to show interest in talks on war in the middle east, the recession or primary debates between Hillary and Barack. This was not on the account of ignorance, but because most rated the news and its persistent promotion of propaganda equally as burdensome. Who needed to hear of war abroad (though sympathetic), when the American government was waging war against us right here in the States through reckless policing and unjust laws.

Recession? Minorities have suffered economically for decades. While the election of America's first black president or female president would prove to be historically groundbreaking and do wonders for the hope of future generations, was hope all we needed? No, what we needed was for America's punishing of its own to end. We needed for the country which spoke of democracy to live up to it. What we needed was for monetary greed to no longer supersede the needs of humans.

The conversations had around the prison were that we needed Obama simply because he was a black man. We needed Hillary because she was the downass wife who stood by the side of a former president, who admitted to puffing Ganja and receiving fellatio from his secretary. Sad, but true. What we needed was someone who was sympathetic to the climate of Americans. What we needed was, as Van Jones stated, "A president willing to be moved and millions of American's willing to do the moving."

My unit was the same as every other across the United States. No prison differed when it came to racial disparities. It was obviously clear that minorities and lower class citizens were being attacked. The overwhelming majority were black faces. The racial disparities were as flagrant as graffiti tinted city trains, trucking through the railways of New York.

In 2007, 37 million people were living in poverty and over 1.5 million people were being housed in prison. The correlation between poverty and prison, race and imprisonment, reverberated like a Rob Bass jam at a 90's block party. What I didn't understand was why everyone was playing deaf? The saddened sounds of set aside souls were conveniently muted. The one who heard and saw couldn't, in good conscience, refuse to act. So the imprisoned continued to be arranged as slaves and nothing more as many covered their eyes and plugged their ears.

My eyes weren't deceiving me. Mass incarceration and its genocidal objective were a bonafide reality. How was it that you and I stood side by side, staring in the same direction, yet identify two separate truths? Does the truth not stand on its own? Prison was not a place filled with happy days, this you must know. It was punitive at its core; picture the punishment.

From 2000 to 2010, drug offenses doubled the incarceration rate. The importance of this was found in the fact that America creates the economical depression. The lot was all but forced into *'by any means';* acts for bread and water. You didn't have a chance in hell when the meat and potatoes were proven to be reserved for the wealthy. It was a sightless search, inescapably steering minorities towards prison. Go to bed hungry and wake up starving, ribs touching. The pros of a good meal outweighed the cons of a life behind bars.

The overcoming of external challenges and conditions were all that mattered. My unit was full of faces that read, *'If the silver spoon next to the lobster and steak was made available to all, most of us wouldn't be here'.* It was pathetic of a country that prided itself on being opportunity-driven yet had more jails than colleges. Together we have been coerced into paying no mind to the systematic repression. Before long America's greed would imprison and enslave entire populations of people. Those not included in this enslavement were a whopping 1%: the wealthy. Today's criminal justice system was not curbing society of criminal behavior and its ills, but returning a race of people to a state which was said to be abolished.

"It is more profitable to catch slaves than to mind the gold." -Marcus Rediker.

Wait, it gets worse. What I saw with my own two eyes day in and day out was the most treacherous truth I'd ever seen. The cold bodied creativeness of a wretched reality; the exploitation of prison labor with not so much as a care for those it profited from. It awakened me to the flipside. Prison wasn't all about punishment. It was also about profit. While we were not literally being driven to cotton fields, the bleeding of our bodies came to be accepted by the general population. Let us thank the United States Constitution and its 13th amendment.

'Neither slavery nor involuntary servitude, except as a punishment for crime whereof the party shall have been duly convicted, shall exist within the United States, or any place subject to their jurisdiction.'

I was haunted by this naivete which had pushed me along with millions to pledge to a flag encompassing the return to labor. Each morning, just before dawn, the air around the prison reeked of exploitation, just as the skies were murky. Inside lived a resounding rumble which erupted routinely as inmates prepared for take-off, already programmed. Whipped senseless till mentally subservient were not them, not us, but we. Prison was also a part of your reality.

When the doors opened, men with ashy faces and sleep in their eyes rushed to '*work*'. No food was in their stomachs, only coffee in their cups prepped to slave. These were your peers. The women coerced into believing their duty was to feed the beast. The same women who were potential Kamalas (Harris) and Michelles (Obama). Men sprinted like marathon runners, rushing to be further marginalized or disciplined for insubordination. These were illustrations of our parents, their parents, and even their parent's suffering. When did the cycle end? To hate slavery was to hate prison.

"Work call!"

The prison intercom roared like a lion pumping fear into the hearts of sheep before the kill. With money as the motive, the first detail announced every single day was Unicor. (Unicor was a government corporation established by Congress in 1934. It was a prison labor program which produced primary goods and supplies for the U.S. military). Nothing moved but the money. Each khaki uniform representing a maximized gain. Prison didn't employ, it exploited: taking advantage of cheap labor through empty wages.

Bearing witness to the machine styled operations of the prison left no question of the monopolized blueprint. It was the reinvention of slavery by criminalizing humans. Penitentiary inmates were 21st-century slaves. All the while the wolves of Wall Street winked, high fived, and celebrated the labor of its captives. Running neck and neck were mass incarceration and mass production. Over the span of a million yesterdays, there was no doubt that prison was a two-headed monster.

Punishment and profit; rehabilitation was what they sold us over the table. Monetary greed made the shameless distribution of excessive prison terms *'cute'*. Our backs were stepped on as the rich got richer. So what do we have? The recycling of citizens duly convicted and punished to involuntary servitude. One monstrous head meant to torment the other to ravage the emotional and psychological properties a man had to call his own. The dangers caused by carceral exploitation swept through our neighborhoods as our bodies made the machine; money, money, money.

Millions of prisoners with no face were the result of a stripped identity, held only as an able body. We were living as *'non-humans'* under the laws of 19th-century plantation politics, working until there was no more work to be done. One had no rights other than being slaves. A disregard for this set of rules landed one in the Special Housing Unit. Rebelliousness was not tolerated and refusing to be subservient was indeed rebellious.

The consequences were not always administered by the administration. The most consequential piece of prison labor, or the refusal of labor, occurred when this work conflicted with the prison population. There were many occasions where the prison was placed on total lockdown. Prisoners were confined to their cells for twenty-four hours a day until its completion. We were fed dry cereal and lunch meat repeatedly. Showers were had every 72 hours. There was no use of the telephone, e-mail service, and no visits.

Institutional memorandums were slid beneath the cell doors advising the general population that all were to remain locked down until further notice. No sooner than these memorandums were passed out, you could see from your cell window lines of prisoners being led to the prisons Unicor. Set aside, though as slaves, under the guise of being top tier inmates, their cell doors were opened. Though they were made to *'work'* any time they were out of the cell, it was indeed a reprieve from the bite of being locked behind a door. Nearly all privileges which had been snatched from the remaining population were returned to these workers: an impish reward for not disturbing their riches.

The danger these inmates were placed in was passed over. There were no issues in reaching this conclusion. In America, a dollar trumped humanity any day. Proof of this insensitivity towards prisoners was the men who had been stabbed, beaten, and denounced by their peers, which was a death in itself. This included those who had lost their lives after being thrown in the deep end of a pool, where right was wrong and wrong was right.

It was just another of the prison's methods of self-destruction. Refuse to be a slave while your fellow brothers in arms remained locked down, and be sent straight to the jail inside of a jail. Refuse to embrace an *'us against them'* mentality by accepting work, and be confronted by a reality that contained three or more convicts. This confrontation would include prison made shanks and blood lost by the liter. This was what you encountered being in a system that rushed judgment and punishment, if your actions differed from their doctrine. All the while you'll hear, *"We'll protect you!"* from your captors. Protection? Hilarious! This was what the countless unspoken for prisoners who were assaulted daily, on average, thought.

To place one's life in known danger was a criminal act; an act that our criminal justice system swept under the rug. Instead of blocking the pleas for help by the exploited, their ears were full of the sounds of money machines. This single shade of prison gave a new perspective on forced labor. To do or die, literally. Prison attire made you an instrument; a link in the penal institution's production machine.

The prison labor did differ from what I imagined. It differs from old school movie portrayals of prisoners with hammers in hand, pressing license plates around the clock, or digging for God knows what on a chain gang. Although these demeaning deeds grew more sophisticated, they remained just as strenuous. Prisons have complex jobs like plumbing, landscaping, and general maintenance. In addition to compound focused labor, there was the existence of work through subcontractors. These were created by corporate investors who had pumped mountains of money into mass incarceration, only to retrieve worlds of wealth from its prisoners.

As a federal prisoner I was amongst the highest paid in the United States penitentiary. Our earnings could reach up to $1.25 an hour; "Look, mama, I made it!" Understand that this Unicor and its additional nickel and dime allure attracted the majority of federal prisoners. The staff ate this up and played on this thirst, as if it was a privilege to have your physical body dominated for pennies. Money wasn't the root of all evil. The lengths in which many went to attain it was.

Envision Unicor as a large factory; rows on top of rows, inmates elbow to elbow, and military fashioned materials stacked in piles from floor to ceiling. There were sewing machines galore. You could hear the loud sounds of needle's punching thread through the fabric in fired succession. Prisoners wiping sweat from their foreheads while stepping mightily on sewing machine pedals to meet their quotas. Correction officers peered over their shoulders like drill sergeants. Chow time was your only break. Even then quotas had become so demanding, men refused lunch, curbing their appetites with coffee. They were organized robots.

While prisoners were not absent-minded to the abuse, many felt that their backs were against the wall; most with little to no outside support. Already up against best friends who tell prisoners' wives *"He's only using you"* or mothers-in-law who spewed *"You can do better"* to their daughters. Men swallow their pride *here* to save face *there*.

All around were men like me, working and slaving as if we'd never had nothing; the system tugging at our short chains for we were treated like dogs. Michelle Alexander, the author of The New Jim Crow professes, *"The system of mass incarceration has birth a vast new under caste. A permanent second class status."* I couldn't have agreed more. However, when you experience the blatant disregard for the most basic human rights, this labeling needed to be questioned. Second class status was actually a step up from what we endured here. A look inside the prison system would leave you speechless. No words gave justice. My first and only encounter with this unmoving slave ship known as Unicor arrived later into my bid.

****

The year was 2009. A Washington, D.C. comrade of mine, Sam "Dogface" Gaither, and I discovered ourselves stumbling down the corridor from Unit B-2, having just chugged a gallon or so of jailhouse hooch. Hoping to not get '*pulled over*' by wandering C.O.'s, we ran directly into the unit manager: an uptight suspender wearing Mr. Rogers type. We were doing everything in our power to ride the wall as he passed, certain that if he smelled the sweet scent of rotted fruit, potatoes, and sugar, the hole would be our next stop. Successfully we made it past when in the distance my unit manager called my name.

"Butler!" he yelled, his face a clear sign that he was relishing in the moment. A joker's smile creased his lips. "I just completed your referral packet to the SMU."

The SMU was a Special Management Unit that was newly opened. It housed prisoners who were said to require additional management. What exactly had I done to warrant the submission? I was uncertain. My institutional jacket was far from extreme, in comparison to the incidents most had been involved in. The thing was, I was not like most. Just as I'd been placed in New Jersey's State Prison Management Control Unit years prior, they had never truly wanted me to walk a compound minus close supervision.

As a means to combat the SMU, I along with a few of the homeboys, concluded that I should try to slide in Unicor to stay out of the way, and maybe convince the '*people*' that I did not need the undesirable send-off. With my plan in motion, a trusted comrade pulled a few strings and secured me an interview. Following deliberations and the fast traveling vibrations of the Unicor staff, I was hired.

This was just what I needed. I was under no terms a model inmate, nor could I say I desired to be. However, as a set up for failure, I was to be given a chance with zero opportunities to misstep. Credit was to be given to the staff's accurate assumptions. I was not a man opposed to an honest living. I would accept the grit, the grind, and the struggle that came with a nine to five.

On the streets, that fast buck came with a trail of invisible mountains one would never ascend. Until we began caring less for the glittering gold and more about our honorable presence in the home as fathers, be us rich or poor; the exploitation of prison would always thrive. My defiant mindset was a direct response to this truth.

'This Unicor was not work, and I, nor any other prisoner, was no employee. This was slavery in a warehouse, which along with the production of military goods, produced slaves.'

This was proof that we were willing to accept anything, if we allowed the distribution of a couple of coins to steer us away from the big picture. Therefore, in this instance, we were the ones being hustled. *"Can't knock the hustle,"* said Jay Z.

From the moment I stepped my black steel-toed work boots inside of Unicor, I knew I was out of bounds. Still, I pushed through with so many thoughts breaking my peace of mind. Above the factory's discord, I heard one voice and saw one face; a Caucasian man in a suit and tie; a gel haired supervisor throwing insults like grenades at working prisoners. There was no doubt he knew the lot needed this work; therefore, his verbal rants would be overlooked.

"Hurry up with those fabrics before I have you back in the kitchen flipping burgers."

"I hope your grandmother didn't teach you to sew like that."

Fearful of what a verbal confrontation could create, most kept quiet. As if slaving for wages that quantified as zilch was not hostile enough. Coursing through my veins was a burning sensation of anger, while the blood in my eyes boiled red hot. An explicit hatred was consuming me. Not a racial hatred, but a fiery hatred for the ignorance which moved through a man's mind, causing him to degrade another.

"Lock us up and work us to death. I'm irrelevant to society. That's what you're telling me. The penitentiary will only hire me." -Kendrick Lamar

Passing through the Unicors metal detector, I was met by my Section Supervisor and the nefarious cycle of mistreatment continued. Amid the sightseeing, he repeated the phrase, *"This place.."* while motioning with his hand as if revealing something marvelous, *"… is a business and not an atmosphere for fraternizing."* In addition, he instructed me on what machine I would run and what would be my daily quota: seventy-five tags pricing at $0.15 cents each. He was leading me from one area to the next like a proud parent. He continued to ramble on until his tongue slipped.

"I know who you are."

During this period, word was circulating around the jail that I had no qualms with pulling a move like Bishop did Raheem in 'Juice.'

Regardless of how frivolous this information was, and what he thought he knew, I knew exactly who I was and being a '*shot caller*' was not it. What I did enjoy was the fact that despite my khaki-colored uniform, I could shake the prison just as much as he could and he knew it. Tewhan Butler was indeed recognized by the powers that be. Yet the recognition was not a product of my being free.

Overall, my section supervisor gave off the appearance of a man of understanding. Unfortunately, his job description ran with the secret motivations of prison policy. This stint in Unicor was expected to be short-lived. Nevertheless, a mere forty-eight hours after being hired, I quit. There I sat busting my ass sewing velcro on polyester strips the size of my pinky finger when over the intercom my name rang out loudly.

"Butler, report to the front office!"

It was reminiscent of my days in middle school when the principal desired to scold me for misbehaving. Immediately upon my arrival, trouble could be sensed. To my right stood my Section Supervisor and his '*understanding*'. Directly in front of me, sitting behind his wood furnished desk, sleeves rolled up, tie loose, and a smug look on his face was the factory chief, '*Mr. Insult*' himself. He was repulsive.

"So, how do you like your new job, Mr. Butler?" The sarcasm in his voice was clear as the waters of the Caribbean seas.

I began examining my surroundings. Feeling ambushed already I opted for a short and direct response. "It's aight."

In my entire life, I'd never been more deceitful. What I really wanted to say would have removed that '*holier than thou look*' right from his face. What he needed to hear was in spite of a man's crime, his time, his lack of wealth, or his riches, he was still a man. Maybe a man who had exhibited errors, but nevertheless a man. His self-assured status didn't afford him the right to walk around with his ass on his shoulders. I also should've reminded him that only a coward oppressed those who were clearly struggling.

"So you really enjoy the work here?" he questioned again.

Was this a trap? Was it a game of cat and mouse where the chase was to be cut short? From where I stood, other than betraying my own conscience, I had done no wrong. Yet there was no mistaking; the stage was set. Readying my mind for the discomfort of the hole, my wrists began to chill anticipating the iciness of cold cuffs.

Experience had taught me that consequences can find their way into your life, even when there are no wrongs.

With my eyes alone, I replied. A thousand words spoken in silence. Feeling himself losing ground, he reached behind his desk, bringing out a clear plastic bag containing a hundred or so polyester strips. "If you like your job, why have you been trashing my hard earned money?" he rebutted in an accusatory tone.

Money? Hard earned? Did he not know the exploited labor of those like me who put food on his table? This entire charade was a circus.

My *'understanding'* section supervisor stood by tight lipped, avoiding eye contact. He was refusing to make it known that he was the one who had directed me to trash whatever was left over, following the fulfillment of my quota.

At this point, an explanation was of no use. If my section supervisor was too afraid to defend his own instruction, what leg did I have to stand on? They didn't want me in Unicor, and this was evidence enough that I didn't need to be there. With my frustration building, and tired of the games, I asked a question. "Am I fired?"

"No! Report back to your station!"

Turning hastily, I placed my hand on the door handle to leave. Before I could disappear into the center of nowhere, the chief supervisor, believing himself to be the victor of this mental trial of strength, stopped me in my tracks.

"Butler, I'll be watching you!"

If this was a game of chess, I had just been *'checked'*. Whatever the result of my actions, I was proud to accept. The maintaining of my self-respect far surpassed the darkest portion of prison. My conviction was as mighty as Tommie Smith and John Carlos. Physically, the chains were strapped tight; however, only I commanded my mental abilities. With a smile resembling our late great Nelson Mandela, I spoke up. "I quit!" Checkmate!

In those times, a part of me desired deeply that my fellow prisoners would hear me, see me, and raise hell. That we would build upon these actions and move. Though my actions were not politically driven, political awareness was a necessity. We were championing the opposition by failing to take corrective action. Prison was destroying the best parts of our being. We were strangling ourselves with our own hands. In our minds, we needed to demand freedom. We were sitting back soundlessly accepting the abuse we couldn't afford to stand for. What we needed was not a call to violence. We needed a Lawrence Fishburn type holler like in the movie School Daze:

"Waaaaakkkkkeeeee uuuppp!"

Were we not offending our ancestors by becoming slaves to our own ignorance? Until we woke up, we would forever be captives of this non-judicial system.

My final day in Unicor did not manifest a mass demonstration. There lived too deep within our souls self individualist ideologies. This machine was good at what it did. In both body and mind, the system had curbed rebelliousness. When lacking in consciousness you can never convince a man that one hundred pennies were the same as a single dollar, when he knows not the value of life. Until we identify that, *"the same fire which keeps us warm was also burning down our villages"*- Elon Musk, we were doomed.

The chains of carceral labor and America's fascination with wealth would surely continue to lock and stock its citizens. The deprivation of economic stability pushes out thoughts of morality, and so we either submit and be chained or rebel and be chained.

" Our change in status from an article of moveable property to untrained misfits on the labor market was not as most think a change to freedom from slavery, but merely a change to a different type of slavery." -George Jackson

Over the years, I would sit down with elders resembling an old campfire gathering. Like an eager child hungry for an earful of truth, I'd listen to how generations of prisoner's sought to ignite the spark which would set fire to this calloused system. Sick and tired of being sick and tired, all burdened by a duty to do something, we knew something had to be done. Despite this instance where I felt I was left alone by my comrades, there were those who had chosen to act. History had shown sit-ins by prisoners and hunger strikes. In prisons, like Angola and Alcatraz, there were actual hostile takeovers. Being tortured as a consequence of a crime was said to be unacceptable in this country. Nevertheless, the beatings continued. We listened to politicians express their desire to make society safer, while still exploiting prisoners.

'What we don't see, we don't know.' This was their policy. A heart soiled by hate, promotes hatred regardless of the fancy wordplay.

The system's scheme to attain wealth was no surprise and the lengths in which they were prepared to go was no mystery. Since the signing of the emancipation proclamation, our government has kicked out billions of dollars to covertly reinvent slavery. I seriously doubt our country would have the highest rate of incarceration, had these billions of dollars been directed at social advancement, increasing opportunities for people to grow, as opposed to landing in prison. In 2013, it was quoted that the average annual cost of federal incarceration was over $4,000.000.000. Now that was a lot of zeros.

The prison campfire of elders who shared these truths were no fools. Who knew better than their exploited selves? Standing beside these men, having myself been forced in as an unwilling participant in the systems process of exploitation, my comprehension of what was taking place made me Ph.D. qualified.

Stage 1 - Arrest
Stage 2 - Throw away the key
Stage 3 - Strip identity and call it reform
Stage 4 - Pose as saviors by awarding pennies for pay
Stage 5 - Exploit, exploit, exploit!

Chapter 4

Welcome To The Big House

In 2010 and with Unicor behind me, a Special Management Unit referral was pending. I sat among the first to be submitted to the SMU, so being rejected was highly unlikely. The SMU was up and coming. To justify the finances they extracted from prison Adult Continued Education, there lived a dire need to fill beds. As a result, infractions that typically would have led you to the hole for thirty days max, now made you eligible for SMU designation.

In my mind, it was only a matter of when I would be snatched off the yard and forced to face the music. Referral hearings were more about formalities than truth-seeking. Your designation packet contained '*confidential findings*', which made successfully challenging your acceptance as slim as Kendall Jenner. The SMU was recently opened so I had little to compare it to. However, I knew it came with nothing more than a pot to piss in. Additional comfort was out of the picture, let alone in the frame. Whatever it was, I imagined that if I applied mind over matter, I would be okay.

A few weeks following Super Bowl Sunday, New Orleans vs. Indianapolis, the prison went on lockdown after receiving word that the prison population was planning to set off an organized strike. Monday was to be the day, and everyone appeared to be ready. Minimal food had been passed around and the only thing left to do was '*stand up*'.

Unfortunately, before day one of the strike, someone had spilled the beans to the prisons' administration. Instead of the doors opening at their scheduled 6 a.m., we remained locked down. The next time my door opened, three officers were standing on the other side with clicking cuffs.

Bang! Bang! Bang!

"Butler, get dressed!" demanded the officers.

"Where am I going?" I asked.

Leaving the cell unescorted during a lockdown was a set up for failure. The last thing you wanted to do was be seen conversing with staff alone, moments before an unfortunate set of events regarding another inmate popped off. You would indeed be the culprit. This rule had been relayed along with the others upon my arrival and these rules were not to be broken.

"To the hole."

"The hole? For what?" I was baffled that they were coming to get me.

"We don't know. The L.T. sent for you. Jones, pack his stuff."

At that moment I knew I would not be returning. Fighting was of little use. When they sent for you, they sent for you. A failure to comply resulted in gas masks, pepper spray, zip ties, and a big can of kickass. Understanding the odds were not in my favor, I turned to my cellie, Drop G. We'd been together for the past two and a half years, sharing everything from sugar to shit. If he was not my brother beforehand, surely our shared struggles helped to solidify our bond.

Staring at him, I found myself holding back tears. In prison we lose so much and here it was we were losing that camaraderie that only came by way of brotherly love. At this moment I envisioned everything I'd ever lost: family, friends, and love. Now the system and its unpredictable ways were taking away my comrade. Knowing this would be the last time we would see each other until we regained our freedom, I turned and mouthed the words, *stay dangerous*.

Entering the hole and frustrated at the turn of events, I decided to jack the cuffs. This was a tactic where the inmate turns around, lets the C.O. uncuff a single wrist, then quickly spins around before the C.O. can uncuff the other, leaving the inmate with the cuffs in his possession and both hands free. Typically this wasn't my style. I was more laid back, but there were instances when drastic times called for drastic measures.

Taking the good with the bad was the true sign of a man. However, on this day, I felt alone. There was no way a physical altercation with the staff could amount to more pain than what I was already feeling. Perhaps they would do me a favor and beat me out of my misery.

"Suit up!" I yelled, pacing back and forth, readying myself for what was to come. I was telling each officer that arrived at my cage to bring it on.

In the past, I had deemed this approach by convicts senseless, but in the heat of the moment, you feel like you need to do something, even when the cards were not in your favor. I have watched staff beat inmates bloody as they punched and kicked them. *'Fuck it'*, I thought.

"Butler, give us the cuffs!" The officers had neither sympathy or empathy in their tone; they stood emotionless. For them it was a job only. Who was I to stand in the way of their paychecks?

"Suuuiiittt uuupppp!" I yelled, tears nearly spilling from my eyes. I had convinced myself that more pain was the only remedy to the anger I was already experiencing.

"This is the last time! Give us the cuffs!" the officer shouted.

Since my arrival at Big Sandy, I was privileged enough to have had a shoulder to lean on, a listening ear, someone who understood my struggle at least to a degree. Now that I was being shipped out to another prison and being separated from my comrade, the pain of prison life intensified almost instantly.

With squinted eyes, furrowed brows, and a tucked bottom lip, I moved to the back of the Bullpen. "Fuck you!" I said storming off.

Since the officers were used to inmates conforming, I was sure to be met by the L.T. and his gang. First, I stood there for a half-hour, then one hour with nothing but time to think. Something at the moment I didn't need. I stood there in the back for another two hours, then three, with my energy subsiding. Just standing at the ready with a single cuff attached to my wrist, dozing off on my feet.

"Butler, what's going on?" Standing in front of the Bullpen was the shifts L.T.

"What am I back here for L.T.?" I asked. A simple answer would suffice, but answers in most instances came in the fashion of disrespect.

"You've been designated to the SMU. Now cut the shit and give me my cuffs." The L.T. demanded.

"L.T., you know this some bullshit." I yelled.

"I can't say it isn't. I tried to put in the word, but it's above my pay grade. You know the game. I'm just doing my job."

At what point the L.T. stopped believing he was a part of *'they'*, I don't know. He was for sure a piece of the puzzle of prison that oppressed us all. From the warden, captain, officer, architect, and visiting hall vendors, all the way down to the nurses, who dismissively passed out psych medications at pill line, they were all a part of this.

We were those whose dreams were being killed. In the end, I gave up the cuffs and was sent to my cell pending transfer to the SMU.

On the way to the hole, the filth hit me like a body shot from a heavyweight. Filthy, chaotic, and drama-filled. This was the hole. The air reeked of assholes and elbows. The scent violent, and the noise deafening. From sun up to sun down men yelled and screamed on the doors, discussing everything from sports to Sanaa Lathan. Old-timers sang oldies but goodies at the door, as inmates yelled for them to sing the songs which reminded them of Jill before she went up the hill with Jack and never came back. Bedsheets were ripped and tied to plastic soap packets and slid down the tier, passing leftover food and contraband. We called this *'fishing'*. Others, for recreation, threw feces, tossed piss, set fires, and masturbated to female officers and nurses.

The lighting was dim, the food cold, the sink covered in spittle, and the toilet shit-stained. Men caught up in drama slung threats from one cell to the next with every intention of making good when the opportunity presented itself. Some swapped cells, others manipulated rec cages. Though the Special Housing Unit known as the hole represented segregation, men still got touched. The hole, be it boredom, broken spirits, or abatement of one's wit, ran high on havoc.

A few months passed, and though I had been designated to the SMU back in January, there was no shortage in bed space. So in the middle of March, I found myself stalking the next bus to Lewisburg as if I was headed to Montego Bay. On the morning of the day, I rushed and sparingly brushed my teeth, lightly washed my face, rushed to the door, and called for the C.O.

"I'm ready!"

****

Five o'clock in the morning, I sat shackled and black-boxed inside of U.S.P Big Sandy's Receiving & Discharge. I was not alone. Amongst me sat an assortment of men of all colors: black, white, and brown, all belonging to what we call on this side of freedom, 'Cars'. There was no mystery to where we were headed and though most wouldn't admit it, you could sense the fear; fear of the unknown. The fear that arrives every time the Bureau Of Prisons decided to drop you in the middle of nowhere. With forced attempts at silencing the fear, everyone talked and seemed to get along, but only for the moment. It wouldn't be long before gang affiliations severed ties and racial tensions, shattered friendships, and city laws created animosity. These were prison politics.

After being handed our brown bags full of bologna, cheese, and fruit, that we struggled to eat through the waist chains, we were led to the prison bus otherwise known as the '*Blue Bird*'. A two-hour ride delivered us along with hundreds of other prisoners to Lexington, Kentucky airport, though our flight wouldn't be courtesy of Delta Airlines. What awaited us was a plain white plane with tape on its wing. Traded here, swapped there, dragged here, and carried there; it was people from all over the world, locked up!

No need for crying. I had tattooed tears now because my eyes refused to shed them anymore. This trip was a one and done. Normally you were dropped in Atlanta for a few weeks, flown to Oklahoma, and then chartered to your destination. Lucky me, my next stop was Pennsylvania. Two and a half more hours and then I was there.

Welcome to the big house U.S.P. Lewisburg, Special Management Unit. A federal penitentiary converted into a max custody institution to house America's most dangerous. It was located in the rural area of Pennsylvania, surrounded by miles of grass, cows, and Amish folk. On the exterior, the SMU was unlike any place I'd ever been. Of course, there were your typical barbed wire fences, barred windows and brick walls. The differences were as evident as the raised hairs on the back of my neck. Once we drove past the '*wall*' of the prison, normally there would be a clear passageway for inmates to walk up and down the compound. Now the once empty space was filled with mile-long rows of metal cages to hold men in the likeness of dog kennels.

They were 12 x 12 boxes of steel. Inside these '*recreational*' cages were six men, all dressed in orange two-piece uniforms. From inside the bus I could hear the military-styled cadences.

"One, two, three! One!"

They were exercising from one cage to the next; the military-style workouts and cadences I would later learn to be a show of rebelliousness. A thing that was done to make the staff aware that we had not been broken. In fact, most of the men who entered the SMU would later leave more dangerous, more violent, and more determined to stand up against authority, despite the consequence.

With the exception of Florence Colorado's ADX unit, the SMU was *'it'*. Survive here and you could survive anywhere. Everything the federal system could throw at you in terms of oppressive conditions, resided within this cemented enclosure. To hear men speak of committing their next infraction as a means of going to ADX, simply so they could escape the SMU, was telling enough to the thought's men possessed concerning this place. Hell was here, and the effects compared to none. Mentally draining, sickening amounts of weight loss in short spans, rash covered flesh, eyes yellowed, and thinning hair. Spiritually, some stopped praying, unable to find a mode of silence to worship.

The connections between inmates and family were heavily strained. Those who still had someone to call their own were robbed of any form of compassion from the outside world after their stay. The time in the SMU was too tough. The struggles of hearing from a loved one via phone twice a month wasn't enough to hold together the pieces. The delayed mail only created greater conflict. Feelings of resentment from family towards prisoners often arose by way of the SMU. This was their design to break everything.

Many men have been mandated to the SMU for institutional infractions and have never touched general population again or, at least, in one piece. At first glance, as I was shackled and leg-ironed alongside fifteen other troublesome inmates, I knew this was a place where the ground always appeared to be caving in. What a filthy place. Hygienically speaking, you showered once every 48 hours for a span of 10 minutes. You were allowed to purchase three bars of soap every 14 days and groom yourself once a month.

In terms of the intentional ill-judged disasters that cost lives, inmates were thrown into pits, cages, and cells with men who had nothing to lose and everything to gain, in regards to prison reputations. The more violent a prisoner could be, the more his reputation grew. Each inmate who attacked another considered the act as retribution to a system that left them for dead. There were stabbings, beatings, and cells set on fire. This place was dangerous, to say the least. All this I was able to process from the outer decor. So what would *'life'* be like once processed and entered into this place? The SMU was indeed something different.

The happenings here preceded one's arrival. Stories tended to travel to and from penitentiary to penitentiary. As I sat on the bus I could feel the tightening of my chest, the quickened pace of my heartbeat, and the moistness in my palms. No one was safe here. Inmates and guards alike sought to destroy the spirit of any whom they came across that didn't serve their cause. The unknown wasn't what one feared, for all knew exactly what awaited. Danger!

"Listen up and listen up good. When I call your name, you step to the front of the bus. Any move other than the one I tell you to make and we'll show you exactly what the rest of your stay will be like," shouted the L.T. from the front of the bus.

Mentally, I sat deep in thought, unaware that we had even stopped. Just outside the federally funded bus stood correctional officers suited in riot gear; think L.A., Baltimore, and St. Louis. The officers stood there with their nightsticks firmly gripped in their hands and venomous looks in their eyes that were shielded behind helmets. It was pure hatred. This wasn't a job; this was personal. This was the place where they taught us lessons with physical force and no one dared come close enough to hear the screams.

"Ignoring your neighbor won't help him, but helping yourself, just like the devil himself, humph." -T.I.

Once ushered into the folds of Lewisburg's SMU, all fifteen of us remained shackled and leg-ironed. We were then placed in individual holding cells. They dared not mix us up. The federal system had what they like to call *'separations'*. It was a warning marking prisoners who should not be placed together at no cost. Though this *'separation'* oftentimes gets lost in one's file, here at the SMU, at least for the first few hours until we were processed, these *'separations'* would have to hold up.

The procedure for processing flew by in no time. They couldn't wait to lock us behind those doors, wishing we'd vanish from the face of the earth. Amid the processing, the unforgettable thing was not the stares by other prisoners, the threats by staff, or the quiet that rang loud and true, but the sight of a miniature monkey in a black and white jail suit, shackled and sitting atop the officer's desk. Then it hit me, the correlation of the term *'inmate'*, and *'nigger'*. The inmate was the house nigger. The convict was the field nigger.

I understood that being regarded as either was unacceptable. Yet, when choosing a lesser evil, the *'house nigga-inmate'* term was below the barrel bottom. We were not speaking of the term *'n.i.g.g.a'* as the form of endearment used by many African Americans within the confines of urban society. No, we were speaking in terms of 'nigger'; slave owners, whips, and chains. The term utterly affiliated with disdain.

This new term *'inmate-nigga'* was birthed in the wake of prisons and today's mass incarceration. This term had just as much to do with class as it did race. The cultural and socioeconomic undertones could be felt through such gestures as monkeys in prison suits. It was felt just as much as when officers yelled through prison corridors, screaming rap songs and critiquing the way we *'lived'*; the diction you had to hear with more than just your ears. If viewed without consciousness, the assault could very well be seen as nothing more than conspiracies concocted by a bunch of *'criminals'*, looking for compassion or relief from the harshest of realities. Only if you knew, or do you already?

After the processing and threats from the special investigative officers, they explained their knowledge of my institutional history. They went on to say that they were aware that I'd been *'beefing'* with west coast Bloods. Although their allegations and information had no truth to it, they stood strong on their superior Intel. What they knew, was what they would go with. Whatever the outcome, what was to be, would be.

Down the corridor, still unsure as to what housing block I would be placed on or what it looked like, I was standing in front of the entrance to the infamous G-Block. For some reason G-Block held the most notorious reputation of them all. The remaining units were filled with men with a wide variety of infractions, thus G-Block was *'it'*.

G-block was the originating unit when the SMU first opened. Here was where, for a brief moment in time, white, black, and brown all came together to unite against the staff. This was the result of the oppressive conditions we were forced to deal with upon its opening. Because of these men, small privileges were given, such as radios, batteries, additional phone calls, and grooming access. This made G-Block the place to be.

G-Block was pitch black, except for the glimmers of light shining from the windows of cell doors, as inmates stood staring at you. If looks could kill, all would be dead. I alone was being led down the range, escorted by two officers, and one L.T. black-boxed behind my back. The weight of my netted laundry bag containing my belongings for the next eighteen to twenty-four months was digging into my wrist. In the back of my mind, I wondered who I would be celling with. As we stopped in front of cell #206, there on the opposite side of the door, peeking down at me stood a '*giant*'.

"Where you from?" he questioned.

He was so big that I couldn't make out his entire frame, but his height alone let me know a fight with this one would be one I would not forget.

"I'm Queen Street Bloods!" I said, speaking up, chest flared. There was no room for fear. A scared man was a dead man.

Standing at about 6'5, me around 5'7, we locked eyes, both hunting for some degree of physical betrayal. A quick flinch, a blink of the eye, a lip trimmer. Fear couldn't be masked. Just the same, we sought out the noticeable features of the enemy; a quality needed in order to survive in prison. Where men and women on the outside patiently processed their peers, went on numerous dates, feeling each other out, or spent a lifetime with high school chums, unaware to who they truly were, we, in prison, sought the potential for danger in an instant. If it turned out smooth, everyone was happy, but when it turned sour, there were no shocked faces.

The constant visuals of backstabbing, and backbiting sparked this critical thinking. Maybe this outlook spilled over from the very system which held us, claiming we were guilty till proven innocent. I firsthand understood that this viewpoint often made it difficult to have an honest relationship. Being fearful of betrayal, you just couldn't find the strength to give up all of you. As a consequence, many relationships failed. I was sorry for all those I cheated. Trust, it wasn't me. It was the domineering circumstances that made me emotionally incompetent.

My soon to be cellmate was from the jungles of California. So much for beefing with west coast Bloods. As I stood waiting to enter into the cell, I heard numerous voices yelling out.

"Ayo, Mass?!" The men behind these voices I knew not, thus I would be sure to find out. To be aware was to be alive, and I had every intention of leaving prison in one piece.

"What's poppin?" I responded.

I desperately wanted to know who was behind these voices and doors. If you dared not die in prison, you needed to not get yourself killed. Heightened awareness and vision of the most minuscule features were what kept you breathing. If either my cellmate or I chose to betray the quick agreement once the doors were opened and relocked, and we were uncuffed, there would be little to no time to put out the fire once the spark had been lit.

"Yo, Blood, that's the homie. Let him in," yelled another voice from behind an unidentified door on the range. That was all the go-ahead I needed, before the giant said things were cool and stepped away from the door. Crazily my new cellmate had just been attacked while in handcuffs by his previous cellie. Ironically, the homies had told him the same thing.

"He's good, let him in."

During my stay in the SMU I saw numerous men attacked by their cellmates. They were attacked while they remained in cuffs, thinking the relationship was solid, only to be sneak attacked, and pulverized. The damage not only physical, but to the point where the sound of clicking cuffs paralyzed their movements for the remainder of their lives.

Once inside the cell we both uncuffed without incident and backed into our respective corners like prized fighters. Both on opposite sides of the cell, ready to charge ahead if necessary, despite the word of others.

"What's poppin?" I mouthed.

"What's cracking?" he responded.

His response caused an immediate furrow across my eyebrows. The cultural differences took shape in an instant, and we still had eighteen to twenty-four months to go. Him from California, me from New Jersey. The system didn't hesitate to '*beat*' us both down as though we'd come from the same womb. I was transferred in from

USP Big Sandy, and he from USP Victorville. Filling up the Special Management Unit resembled law enforcement's desire to fill quotas. In 2009, a Bureau Of Prisons alert went out to every federal institution notifying administration of the following criteria.

Designation to an SMU may be considered for any sentenced inmate whose interaction requires greater management to ensure the safety, security, or orderly operation of bureau facilities. This also includes the protection of the public, if the inmate meets any of the following criteria:

- Participated in disruptive geographical group/gang-related activity.
- Had a leadership role in disruptive geographical group related activity.
- Has a history of serious or disruptive disciplinary infractions.
- Committed any 100 level prohibited acts, according to 28cfr part 541, after being classified as a member of a disruptive group.
- Participated in, organized, or facilitated any group misconduct that adversely affected the orderly operation of a correctional facility.
- Otherwise participated in or was associated with an activity such that greater management of inmate interaction with other persons was necessary to ensure safety, security, or orderly operation of bureau, or protection of the public.
- The inmate must have at least 24 months left on his/her sentence.

The troubling aspect of this criteria was all of it. A whopping ninety-nine percent of the bureau inmates fell into a category that made them eligible. How could you escape such vague language? In a matter of months the bureau filled what use to be an entire USP with SMU inmates. I was one. Shocking? I think not!

Now let them give voice to the millions whose potential they shackled by refusing them the opportunity to right their wrongs. Behind a closed door one could do nothing but watch blood trickle down the painted walls of his prison cell. Yet the Special Management Unit was said to be non-punitive. How could it not be when we lose a part of ourselves each waking moment; when each day they leave us trapped?

My physical being present, however my world had long ago been shattered. Where was my room to grow or to find alternatives to violence? There were none. My cell was 8x12, so if I couldn't find it in such a space, then too bad. The outside world would simply believe me to be the one who refused rehabilitation during my incarceration. The system would never admit that prison was nothing more than death. Prison was Derek Chauvin knee on the neck of another black man - Murder.

After the convict ceremony, we paused our conversation. We both took a deep breath, though not relaxed, and attempted to play it cool. When the tension subsided, I was able to step to the door and 'see' who had been calling me. At the door, I quickly learned that it was a comrade named Biggum whom I had done time with back in USP Big Sandy.

Biggum had been on the compound all of seven days when we found ourselves dealing with a situation that was unavoidable. Penitentiary politics often called for action. During the altercation, me, Biggum, and a co-defendant of mine found ourselves assaulting another inmate who was under the false impression that he would no longer run with the homies. It wasn't that we didn't want homies to progress, or move on but, while in prison, straddling the fence could get you killed. Everyone took it serious when an individual held the belief of divided loyalties. If you come in with the Bloods, you leave as a Blood. You come in with the Crips, you leave as a Crip. For this reason within the first twenty-four hours, you were to make it clear with whom you were running.

As punches were thrown, blood was drawn and the police came running. In the process of being detained, correctional officers testified that Biggum had taken a cheap shot at one of the officers resulting in a fractured jaw. With so much commotion going on before I could be detained, I slipped off into the crowd, making it back to my unit. As I entered, I heard the unit officer yell.

"Lockdown!"

Suddenly there were bodies rushing to the ice machine, shower, and cells. I was just happy I'd been able to get away, or so I thought. Once secured in my cell, I looked around wondering what additional hardships my co-defendant and Biggum were being taken through. To be accused of assaulting an officer there was definitely a price to pay. We were thirty minutes into the lockdown when an L.T. and two officers stepped to my door.

"Butler, turn around and cuff up."

So much for the grand escape. Within the corridors and the compound there were cameras everywhere and where there weren't cameras there lived what we liked to call 'human cameras'. There were inmates who would cough up information for as little as a book of mailing stamps.

Turning around, I stood still and let the officer cuff me. Once outside the cell, I could see inmates standing in their doorways checking to see what was going on. On their faces were looks of concern, others joy as they would much prefer someone to take a fall so the doors could be reopened, despite what came next for those sent off. In addition, there were looks of disappointment from the brothers who promoted peace.

Inside the L.T.'s office, it was said that I'd given the go-ahead for the assault, though the cameras had not seen me do a thing.

"So, you have your homies assaulting my officers?" shouted the special investigation L.T.

"I don't know what you're talking about. I ain't tell anybody to do anything."

"So you don't run the car for the Bloods?" the L.T. shot back.

"No!" I yelled, attitude detected in my tone.

"Send him to the hole with the rest of them." the L.T. instructed.

As quickly as I came, I was being dragged to the SHU. There had been rumors for years, from one penitentiary to the next, that quite a few 'shot callers' cooperated in one form or another with the administration. My uncooperative stance proved I could not be compromised, and so they sought to lock me up.

This day on the door, as Biggum recanted his trials since we separated, I could hear the obvious pain in his voice.

"Damu, they gave me eighteen."

In my mind, I asked, '*eighteen, what?*' There was no way this could be true. If you wanted to know about the cruel and unusual punishment we faced, this was the definition. He was given eighteen additional years for an alleged assault. Eighteen years was a lifetime. This eighteen meant the birth of a child, the first day of school, middle school socials, high school proms, and graduation. That was so much life to miss. To be black and make it to the age of twenty-one was monumental. To survive eighteen years in prison was unpredictable. These eighteen years meant that our judicial system was sentencing men to time not for rehabilitation, but to time where anything could happen.

As Biggum spoke, my heart hurt. At the time of the incident, he had only a few months before release. If only we could turn back the hands of time. I was unable to respond because of too many feelings and too many thoughts. Again, we had lost to the system. Biggum's eighteen years were my eighteen years. There was no difference between me and him. Of course I couldn't do his time and he couldn't do mine, yet the reality of it all was that on any given Sunday we were all subject to the same fate.

Removing myself from the door, hard to digest this terrible truth, I began to trade stories with my new cellmate. Speaking of the unbearable conditions, he and I prepared for the worst. Despite the program's statement, the time spent in the SMU was undetermined. Each institutional infraction forced one to start anew: what we called '*day one, phase one*'. It was when events such as this occurred that this eighteen to twenty-four month stretch ran on for years. Repeat offenders were common, resulting in a large part of SMU inmates being stuck. Some inmates had every intention of using the security of a locked door to their benefit; others were simply trapped by oppressive officers who got a kick out of treating inmates as 3/5's. Regardless, the conditions were yours to stand up under or crumble beneath.

The following day, I was awakened by death. At 6 am, the smell of pepper spray crept beneath the crevices of my prison door. The familiar, yet unwanted scent instantly brought me out of my stupor. The sounds of concussion bombs were blasting in the background.

Boom! Boom!

"Stop! Cuff up now!" yelled prison guards.

Though I was not able to see what was going on, it needed not to be explained. I understood that within the confines of this concrete jungle the best business was nobody's business. I stayed away from the door and went about my daily routine of hygiene.

Maybe it was the heat, a long-simmering beef, or an early morning argument. I was like the many who now embraced their nightmares because their dreams long ago faded. Before completing my thoughts, as does the calm before the storm, all stopped and there was silence.

Out walked a prisoner as reserved as anything I'd ever seen, covered in blood from head to toe. What was seen in his eyes said it all, and the screams which vibrated throughout the tightly fitted tier confirmed it. Minutes later, a stretcher was pushed down the tier in no hurry. The inmate on top was already blanketed by the sheet which ushered you from this life to the next. I was awakened by death and all I could think about was the sign outside the prison. *Welcome to the big house!*

My days slowly turned into nights and my nights to dawn. Each morning I rolled out of my bed to nothing. All around me stood the worst of conditions; they were like third world. '*How did I get here?*' I asked myself. "Was there anything I could've done differently?" Of course, but a different course of action would not have safeguarded me from this reality. Hardships appeared to be something I was destined to run up against. The question was, "How would I fair?"

The tiny space I was now to call home allowed me only a few feet before I was at my door. I was only able to peek out of the rectangular shaped window that permitted me a view to the blank tier and adjoining cells. This particular prison was constructed in 1932. Its concealed conditions were inhumane and utterly unpleasant. I could have been anywhere, yet here I was.

I took the bitter with the sweet and swallowed that which destroyed me. When I go, will I return to this hellish place? Already I was fearful of the future. The number of those who return continues to climb. First, I needed to make it home. Wall to wall, hardly enough room to shape my physical. I pushed up as if the weight of the world rested heavily upon my shoulders. When I could go no more, I went further, harder. The associated matters which modified my course of development, provoked me to exert the force within. One of the few positive things permissible was staring at the walls to impede the ever-tightening grip of this dully-lit dungeon. While at the door, I could hear the cries of fellow inmates. *'Let me out!'* Although I could place no face, I could tell their sanity was gone forever. What they was going through I knew so well. Had I not been afraid of my cries falling on deaf ears, I too would holler.

Four months passed, and I had become a natural fixture of this unnatural existence. At first glance I thought nothing of the SMU. Now, as I sat here, all but strapped inside my cell, reality began to set in.

"You will eat, shit, and sleep wherever we assign you for the next twenty-four months, gentlemen!"

I was thinking back on those words that were spoken when I'd first arrived. Today I deal with roaches, mice, peeling paint, and vents that were nothing more than holes in the wall. There was a pipe that ran directly through the corner of your cell providing heat strong enough to suffocate. In these few months, three bodies have dropped, all the result of being forced into a cell with enemies. Two men, different walks of life, trapped. Neither daring to close their eyes at night. Panic buttons? There were none. Cries for help go unheard.

Sanity was my last true friend, yet I felt it trying its best to leave me. Isolation was nothing to be played with. I was trying to find the right words to describe this place and this feeling, but it was impossible. This was a place where we fight to maintain our sanity as obstacles, trials, and tribulations were constantly placed before us in an attempt to cripple our social and emotional intelligence. Isolation didn't calm the beast. It was mentally altering; the strain with a coldness at its tips, hardened enough to send chills through the very steel that disconnected us from the free world. Do you know of such a place?

Chapter 5

It Won't Be Long

On the move, I could hear them yell down the tier. "Butler, be ready. We'll be back in five minutes."

I was being transferred to level three, USP Allenwood. *"Damn!"*, I thought to myself. This stretch felt more like a never-ending story, filled with page after page of horror. When I first entered the SMU, I observed acts of pure savagery. Men flawed by circumstance and taking on the characteristics of animals, all for survival. Feeding off one another like vultures, with a look in their eyes we call a *'hunger for more'*.

For many days the same cravings ran through me. My sanity was tested and had become strained. Hearing the words *'pack up'* created a moment of delight. Just as fast as those thoughts and feelings came, they vanished. Death awaited us every step of the way. Nothing was worse than being unprepared. So the split-second smile was quickly replaced with seriousness in short order.

No matter how many times it repeated itself, (belly chained, shackled legs and feet), the psychological degradation never grew easier and would never be acceptable. This passing from one penitentiary to the next contained few others. There were nine prisoners in total. I was certain that all had fought just as I to remain standing erect in the darkness of Lewisburg's cold corner.

The ride there was mere minutes. We rolled away from the Big House Road and entered what resembled that of a college campus. That was if your vision could surpass the barbed wire fences and bright orange that swathed its prisoners. The day was gloomy, the rain trickled down and crashed into the concrete, sobering the moment. That was the story of my life, one full of rain. Whatever was good in my world was constantly washed away by rainy days.

Once inside and lined up in a single file, we were unshackled and *'cut loose'*. Painful was the emotion that overtook me. As the cuffs came off, I felt a sense of freedom. Physically, I was not being held captive to the extreme I came to know so well. Figuring it to be a justifiable feeling, considering that the last eleven months of my life had required the company of iron bracelets, double locked, with a black box and escort. Having been restrained to such extremes, the lightness of the links being removed introduced a pseudo comfortability. Psychologically, this was exactly how we enslaved ourselves, following the abolition of slavery. The chains needed not to be removed, only loosened, and everyone went cheering believing justice had been served.

Levels three and four meant another ten months of being locked behind a door twenty-three hours a day with only one hour of recreation. My reward for making it to this phase was to be let outside to play amongst the uncivilized. The attitude surrounding this place was different. Instead of the arrogant, cocky, and ill-mannered C.O.'s pressing for a reaction that would result in one being gassed, beaten, and four-point restrained, the officers here were on guard, but more respectful. A change you will always notice when the cuffs were removed.

On the unit we had televisions to watch, light workout equipment, and the cells went from 8x9 to 10x10. The decor held brighter paint, the floors were waxed and buffed, and the food came hot. In a place we call, *'hell'*, these light shifts in conditions felt like paradise.

My cellmate was another Damu named Meshack. He was a brown-skinned, stocky Syracuse Orangeman who also believed in brotherly love overriding oppression and destruction. To get through the months ahead, we quickly implemented a study schedule and a workout plan. The exercising of both the mind and body were necessities in one's growth. During the day, we pounded away hundreds of burpees, pushups, sit-ups, and light cardio. In the evening we ripped through pages of military script and self-help material. In the night we quizzed one another on future goals, aspirations, and challenged ourselves on the misaligned concepts of manhood; how since childhood we had been taught that we had to be strong, unbending, aggressive, and relentless. These very things played a part in our being in prison.

Both he and I were fathers, so the time we spent locked inside the cell was more time we spent away from our children. We wondered if we were to speak to our sons and daughters and shared with them the stories which led us here, would they be proud or ashamed? The time to think raised questions about what we wanted for ourselves and those we loved. The outward conditions meant little as our focus was on family and the progression thereof. Before we knew it, though not one day was a breeze, the end was near. In August 2011 we both advanced to phase four.

Without tired legs or breaking a sweat, this stint of solitary confinement was over. Long ago, I'd identified the plot to break my spirit by leaving me strapped in a straight jacket in the darkness of nowhere. I couldn't let that happen. Never! You could put me in a box, seal it shut, liquefy my meals, slide them beneath the door, and leave me no running water, and when my time was up, I would rise. I would rise stronger, sharper, and to my captors' dismay, with a smile on my face.

Since the doctors slapped my baby bottom in 1979 and forced me to scream, I had been well prepared for the pain and suffering this cold world would bring. I was told that a young black man growing up in America wouldn't amount to much; that in order to escape the ghettos grit, one had to do the unthinkable. I knew I'd never be free. So here I was at the back end of 2011 and still chained. Any day now my two year stint in the SMU, filled with monotonous 23 and 1's, was coming to a close. Unfortunately, there was no joy for my departure, only curiosity. See, I was broadening my understanding, re-educating myself to the truth, learning to accept the fact that "Black was King." Being armed with this newfound ammunition made me further susceptible to the extreme acts of oppression brought on by management units far and wide.

Having struggled so much in the belly of isolations darkest places, I, at times, questioned if my birth was the proper decision. My parents were undoubtedly loving, just as much as I love myself. Therefore the peace and freedom I had in the womb, provided the best life I'd ever had. When I was born into this mess of a world, the complications began. Others were disappointed that inner city living and poverty didn't end my life. The resentment was so loud that even with closed eyes I could see the gritted teeth of those determined to suffocate me in prison.

As with the New Jersey State Prison Management Control Unit, and now Lewisburg's SMU, I'd made it. However, repetitive trips to isolation seemed inescapable. Year after year, and with every stumble that sent me on extended stays in solitary, the plot thickened. With my criminal cases, I foresaw the inevitable. In prison, working against me was the fact that there didn't exist any jaws-like music playing in the background to warn when this system, that was run by sharks, was ready to attack, as we prisoners were but blood in the water.

On far too many occasions I had been mistaken by outside prison supporters for not having learned my lesson from continuing to play headless chicken. One acquaintance even accused me of being unwilling to pass the torch. At this point I remembered U.S. prosecutor, Ms. Vashs' statement: *"Mr. Butler sought power for power's sake."*

Of all my supporters, no one considered a criminal justice system administered by unfeeling persons; persons who made an estimate on every living soul imprisoned by nothing outside of their shortcomings. No one pictured the Lucifer-like smiles on the faces of correctional officers when they forcefully locked our iron doors for indefinite periods and told us to, *"Have a nice day."* These continuous trips to solitary were nothing more than a result of my unimproved behavior, or so they thought.

In November, grey skies were appearing as one gigantic cloud. Part of me was still searching for the Olympic sized pools, tennis courts, and golf courses. Since I stepped my shackled feet off that bus in Inez, Kentucky, all I'd seen was sheer terror. I spent two years in general population fighting and stabbing, with a brief Kumbaya moment. Then there was more fighting and stabbing, then Bam! I was thrown behind a steel-clad door. Now the next lap of the race was approaching.

Again, I found myself in pursuit of the penitentiary's dangers. I was told to pack up. My turn had come and I couldn't fill the plastic bags with my property fast enough. For the past twenty months I fell in love with my dictionary, thesaurus, and world almanac. I also had my book of morals and the world's best poets to have ever lived. They had to be boxed up and tucked away until we reached the next prison.

After having my property ready to go, my door was unlocked and opened by a unit officer. There were no intimidating looks and no cuffs. I was free, to a certain degree. In the units day room I joined nine others who had successfully completed the aches and pains that came with the SMU. The date was November 29, 2011. The time was 4:45 a.m.

Only once weekly the penitentiary's rule of absolute silence was ignored and this day was one of them. The ten of us began yelling to those we had journeyed with, who still had to travel through extreme hardships.

"Keep your head up!"

"Stay safe!"

"Remain solid!"

Such words on the inside speak of a man's care for another who struggled. We had those we want to stand beside and those we would fight with to the end. However, the FBOP understood this and separated comrades by putting thousands of miles between them in an attempt to block the brotherly love. Our shouts were returned, then the officer yelled, "Let's roll, men!"

Personally, I couldn't wait to roll. The ten of us followed the footsteps of those in uniform to R&D where we were reminded that we were not free at all.

"One straight line, gentlemen. Now strip!"

"Open your mouth and show me your gums. Now your hands and your nut sack. Turn around and show me the bottom of your feet, the left, now right. Bend over, spread'em and cough. Now put your clothes back on!"

Humiliation to the tenth power. We were not seen as men, but as property.

Following the process, we were thrown into the bullpen to wait for hours. There was nothing to eat but two stale slices of bread, and bologna. There were hunger pains mixed with anticipation and butterflies. We were almost there.

In walked three officers. The clanking of chains filled the room with their noise. One by one we were cuffed, shackled, waist-restrained, and leg-ironed; each with a tightness, numbing one from hands to feet. Again, my mind told me I was almost there.

The bus ride was painful as the iron cuffs dug into my skin with each bump in the road. As a reprieve, I attempted to enjoy the sights. One never knew when the next time the free world would be seen. I cherished each passing car, pedestrian, building, and home. These were some of the small things that were removed from my life for years. I stared out the bus window wishing I had understood then the importance of freedom. It was mine to lose and I had lost it.

Before I knew it, we were pulling up alongside a dozen greyhound buses with escape-proof windows; the interior fitted with bars and gates. The all-white federal plane landed moments later and then out comes U.S. Marshals with shotguns and automatic rifles in hand. The perimeter was heavily secured. We were at Harrisburg's airport, but far away from the fancy jets, and Delta 747's.

The name and number calling began.

"Butler, 26852-050!"

I stepped off the bus and took my place amongst the other men and women dressed in pumpkin seeds, paper pants, dingy T-shirts, and shackles. The sight before me was one I could never have imagined. I was almost there.

We entered the plane and there were hundreds of prisoners packed inside like sardines.

"We're preparing for takeoff. In case of emergency do not panic. Listen to the Marshal's instructions and you will be fine."

A man with his wrists strapped to his waist and his feet chained together could never be fine in case of an emergency.

Now we were in the air. Next stop, Federal Transit Center, Oklahoma City. Whatever was outside was unknown as we landed and pulled up directly to the buildings' terminal. As we exited the plane, we immediately entered FTC, OKC.

Inside, US Marshalls lined the walls of the corridor, which was about half the length of a football field. With bright lights and white walls, the decor resembled that of a mental institution. After we were unshackled, we were handed yet another brown bag containing two slices of stale bread and bologna before we were delivered to the bullpen. There was one steel toilet covered in piss, spit, shit, and no tissue. There was also one sink with years of scum lining the inside. One long wooden bench was bolted to the wall, yet there were a hundred or so inmates inside, all sweaty and musky. After the strip out, the inmates were sent to take photos, medical, psychological evaluations, then back to the bullpen.

Some of us in transit had been designated within 500 miles of home, yet the majority ended up in different time zones. Some of the lucky ones awarded their designations with a cheerful, "Yessssss!" Others held fearful expressions. I wondered if there was a way to count the prisoners whom other than chained treks to state prison or the federal penitentiary, have never traveled more than five miles outside of their respective neighborhoods. The stress and strain placed on loved ones attempting to maintain a close relationship were dismissed. The children who had to wait years for their parents to scrape up the funds to fly across the globe to visit their incarcerated guardian meant little to the system. We were shipped like FedEx packages, though the Federal Bureau Of Prisons claimed no responsibility for the unforeseen damages.

It was 11:45p.m. when I finally reached my cell. Before I was able to situate my bedroll (blanket, sheet, hotel sized toiletries), I was told that I would be leaving in the morning; the morning being 2:45 a.m. Physically I was drained as my body called for sleep. However, knowing that I was almost there, my body wouldn't rest. I was forced to go through the entire process yet again. Prison definitely was not a place of convenience.

During this transitional process, another unforeseen damage was when the Bureau refused to accept responsibility for what could be described as a memory loss. Officers failed to maintain the '*separations*' placed on inmates. This resulted in two being placed in the same vicinity and ending in a blood bath. "We're only human and prone to error," says their unwritten policy whenever someone loses the best of their life. Explain this '*mistake*' to the same child you punished by sending their parents halfway across the world. With mistakes like this happening, you wouldn't think about how many of us would return to SMU. The more important question was how many of us would make it home?

****

At 2:45 a.m. I was back on the plane after squatting, coughing, and basically being humiliated to the core again. I was then informed that I was headed to USP Pollock in Louisiana. I only hoped the flight wouldn't be long. Taking off, the plane went speeding down the runway. A few hours later, we landed back in Harrisburg, Pennsylvania to swap out prisoners like cattle. Leave five here and pick up ten there; all chained and shackled, hopping from one line to the next as the leg irons bit into their ankles. This was fair exchange, a body for a body. When one prisoner exited from one bus, another was to return. After an hour of being swapped, the automatic rifles were tucked away, the buses rolled on and we went back in the air.

Finally, the wooded terrain of Alexandria, Louisiana - United States Penitentiary Pollock. Word around the BOP was that this place was rocking and rolling. It was a non-stop work call. The faint-hearted did not belong, so I prepared to enter with a lion's roar. What came next, I would have to wait and see.

After pulling up to the USP POLLOCK, we were quickly thrust into R&D. Pollock was certainly known for its perpetual uproar. Mentally, I knew exactly what I needed to do to overcome the odds and get ahead in a life which was determined to keep me in last place. However, walking the talk was always simple in one's mind. The actions of the limbs were where we typically struggled. Sitting in R&D, I knew in minutes the true test would begin and, at a time I needed it the most, a sacred reminder came to mind from within the Noble Quran.

"Do people think they will be left alone and will not be tested, simply because they say we believe?"[1]

This Surah was the door to my new beginning. However, Pollock would provide the fork in the road. Pollock was my fourth prison in four years. The process was never one you'd grow accustomed to. In Pollock I was aware that already posted on the yard were men expecting a man resembling a Mass of the old and not Tewhan of the future. My comrades, though in good faith, did not recognize that their expectations were but burdens that would kill me if I was unable to get from underneath them with my integrity intact.

How could I explain to these men who have entrusted me, blessed me with respect, familiarized themselves with Mass, but have never met Tewhan, that I didn't 'want' to change. I 'needed' to change. In order for me to be a true leader, I must walk the talk. I have been following a blueprint drawn by everyone other than me for my entire life. Within my gut there lived a violent rumbling telling me, *"They will not understand,"* and that I would be seen as a *"traitor and a fraud."*

I would be examined through the eyes of a blind man as nothing. When I was at a tender age, full of energy, mentally immature and filled with childish pride, I failed to acknowledge the striking similarities between the streets and the penitentiary. Today I saw

---

[1] Surah Al-Ankabut: 2

more clearly, and what I was seeing was that neither would ever permit a man room enough to be himself.

"Most people adapt to their environment more quickly than they should and they adjust themselves to the situation rather than adjusting their situation to the dreams they have inside." -T.D. Jakes

It's 9p.m. and usually the noise of the atmosphere was high pitched. However, the process of being trafficked through state after state, for days on end with minimal food, had us all exhausted. With my bedroll in hand, I was a single prisoner amongst twenty-three new arrivals who were but a pebble in a sea of millions incarcerated. We were all dressed in karate-styled bus shoes, white T-shirts that were now dirty brown, and ashy faces. The bullpen therapy had ended and now the moment of truth had arrived.

At last we exited R&D. We desperately needed to steal one or two hours of rest before morning because once the doors popped, so did the weasel. As we were led across the compound in a single file, without warning, there erupted an ear-splitting sound.

Boom! Boom! Boom!

The prisoners had begun violently banging on the windows signaling our arrival.

Boom! Boom! Boom!

The screaming of obscenities blared like bullhorns.

"Imma kill you!"

"You fucking punks!"

There was absolutely no humor in this ill-mannered welcoming, yet I cracked a smile while snarling at the C.O. who did little to conceal his smirk. This looked like something you'd see on television., except this wasn't acting. Witnessing these men with their eyes bulging and foaming at the mouth was seriously sobering. They were selling death from their cells for next to nothing. I had taken a quick glance at the men in the line, their nervousness was concealed, and thought for the first time just how dangerous prison truly was.

Taking one deep breath of my own, I got ready.

"OK., let's go!"

In this first night there existed nothing but an eagerness to get to it. The peaceful picture which I envisioned in my mind's eye surrounding my new beginning would more than likely not end so peacefully. Cells were locked and the lights were out!

****

Click! Click!

It was morning and the doors were being opened. Immediately the noise of the penitentiary took flight. Those who had their time in, bopped around with no worries, while the new arrivals stepped with caution. The decrepit decor resembled USP Big Sandy only by way of its arrangement. However, the racial disparities were unmistakable. Again the day-room proved to be a testament that black men in America were being plundered. The unit was composed of men with a darker hue. While our president was black, so was the largest portion of the prison population.

From within the unit, I heard my name called. "Mass, what's poppin'?!"

Turning around I instantly spotted the homeboy, Kizer, from Newark, New Jersey's Avon Avenue. Happy to see a familiar face, I responded.

"Damn, I didn't know you were here. I'm good. What's the verdict on your end? After Big Sandy I thought I'd probably never see you again."

"I can't call it. I went to a medium for a Lil' minute, but that shit wasn't for me. The respect level is on zero. Before I knew it, I was forced to set the tone. Now here I am."

Kizer was about six feet, brown skin, and since I'd known him, he had no problem '*setting the tone*'.

"The homies J.V. from 9th Ave, Slash from Trenton, and Jux Brim from New York, upstairs. They should be on their way down. Meg next door on C-3, and Death, Nutcase, and I.B. from Nebraska down in B-building. It's a few more good homies on the yard. We already knew you were coming, so everybody should be in the chow hall."

Indeed they were. The mandatory meet and greet along with the conspicuous sizing up never grew old. It was repeated at every prison. Once inside the chow hall, I recognized the tension, the separation, the fear in some, and the predatory sense in others. I thought maybe I had an enemy in the midst, so my head stayed on a swivel. No matter the number of familiar faces, there could be no relaxing. Often times the ones to get you were the ones standing right beside you.

The commonplace betrayal throughout the federal system served its purpose in the fact that *'anybody could get it'*. Prison was the streets, only much smaller. One of the first Damus I spotted when I entered the chow hall, mobbing in with his signature Diddy Bop, was Omega Red. The same Omega Red I'd left back in USP Big Sandy the winter of 2009. With only fourteen high custody penitentiaries, one was bound to run into someone from the past. It was another prison dynamic which made a transfer all the more hazardous.

Just like old times, Omega and I picked up where we left off as we exchanged jailhouse ebonics, saying nothing while relaying everything. During our conversation Omega placed both his hands below his waist, almost out of sight, took his right fist and slapped it twice against his open left palm. Continuing our conversation as if I hadn't noticed the gesture (someone was always watching), I responded by swiftly nodding my head up and down. Understanding all that came with my agreement, it was back to the basics. I just agreed to arm myself.

"His only knowledge was ignorance." -Socrates

I only proved to be making my life more difficult. I couldn't ignore the looming threat posed by one of America's bloodiest penitentiaries. The agreement to arm myself was not a B-Role performance by a pretend gangsta and definitely not a search for trouble. The weapon was for one purpose and one purpose only - protection. Making it home of my own free will or being shipped in a pine box were my primary motivators.

I had not forgotten about new beginnings. However, I could remove the possibility of walking out of their doors in one piece, if I were to close my eyes and pretend it wasn't Bloody Pollock. From the chow hall, the unit, recreation, the yard, education, and the law library, there was spilled blood everywhere. This was how the system rewarded me. I survived USP Big Sandy, Lewisburg's SMU, and now I needed to outlast Pollock. Every night I was forced to fight against death that was waiting just around the corner.

When twenty-four hours had passed and my tan khakis were pressed, my boots were strapped tight, my knife was tucked, and there was nothing left to do but run the race against time, it was on. Ironically, I had grown accustomed to the danger, yet I still felt faint when learning of truths. Truths such as the 1799 penitentiary act and how this act paved the way for modern-day prisons. This entire cataclysmic system had been around for over two hundred years, predicated on the basis of minimizing minorities.

The hard-pressed politics meant to warehouse African Americans and people of color was apparent. I could literally see the hatred on more than just the interior design of the prison. The canceled trade-funding, the discontinued college courses, and the nonexistent reentry initiatives; all screaming of the system's prejudiced hostility.

When playing the yard, I witnessed hundreds of men exercising, playing basketball, walking the track or simply standing around doing absolutely nothing. It became more apparent why prison was more common than college and why recidivism rates were jumping out of the gym like Lebron in his prime. Repression wasn't reform, but shouting this was like singing to the choir. The setup of days like this proved that the school to prison pipeline was working to perfection. The further dispossessed educational outlets became, the more secure our placement as second rate citizens would be.

If '*light is said to surmount darkness, knowledge the ruler of ignorance*', then why did our justice system isolate, oppose to educate? What was issued to citizens breaking the law was not justice. The sentencing to prison time does little to reform and rehabilitate. Men didn't come home from prison stints twenty pounds heavier and full of muscle, as though they'd shattered every weight in the gym because they aspired to be bodybuilders. It was a result of being put in a place that placed little emphasis on growing the mind.

Prison officials laughed out loud as men walked around bolder chested, flat stomached, and buff armed. In America, among the ruling class, '*might is right*'. Those who held no political power would always be wrong, subject to unbalanced laws, and be fit for the many prison cells built in this country. So, bench-press 465lb, curl 100lb dumbbells, and do 600 squats and this system would still find a way to beat you down.

"Damn blood, you aight?" asked Omega.

"Yeah, I'm straight!" I returned, not even realizing I had zoned out.

My thoughts were something I preferred to keep my own. Hopefully Omega hadn't spotted my fleeting attentiveness. Something was alive in me and prioritizing the things in my life, awakening me to the true nature of my surroundings: prison, its officers, and gun towers compared to cotton fields, slave owners, whips and chains. I could see today the correlation between then and now. To the author of '*Black Ice*' Loraine Cary, let me be the first to tell you that I understand completely when you speak of the insipid confidence of the many who relish the notion that '*might is right*'.

"Blood, grab that real quick and lets hit the chow hall," said Omega.

Feeling for the needle pointed ice pick tucked by my scrotum, I nodded. "I'm ready when you are."

Consistent within the penitentiary was the lack of choices. However, the choices I did have, I chose the wrong ones.

During the quick trip to the chow hall, things began to come to a head. After meeting up with the homies, in typical fashion, we grouped together walking and talking. We were exiting the kitchen, when out of nowhere, a temper flaring administrator stepped directly in my path. In his eyes was a lingering hostile glare. He held the look of a matador and I was his raging bull.

"You Butler?" asked the matador. It was more of a statement than a question.

Like a raging bull kicking up dust before the charge, I snapped back. "Yeah, I'm Butler!"

The old matador felt the prison was his ring and my reply was the challenge he'd been waiting for. As though disgusted with my presence, he looked me over. He then scanned the group of unbending Damus with me watching the '*show*,' refusing to be defeated.

"Well Butler, I don't want you in my jail."

Misunderstanding was placing us worlds apart because I didn't in the slightest want to be here. Prison was no place for a man. Man's evolution would forever be stunted as a result of these bars. Society's glass ceiling was replaced by stone walls and spiked fences. In his mind's eye, I was not a man. The chains had reduced my being, made me less than, and for that he wanted nothing more than to prove he could rule my person.

This entire spectacle was motivated by ideas of hatred. Contrary to my struggles and today's shackles, with dignity was how I was raised, and with dignity was how I would meet my Maker. I wouldn't run from 'might' like our elders, who were forced to run from fire hoses, rabid dogs, and overzealous police squads. Instead, my fight demanded that force be met with force.

With that in mind, I stood my ground. My stance would not deter those in power from manufacturing incident reports or pseudo criminal acts. It wouldn't stop them from dragging one to the hole and losing them there, although there was a fearlessness that still needed to be exercised. After a moment of darting eyes, zero blinking, and no room to budge, I turned and walked away. I exited the chow hall with certainty that the unresolved issue would be reignited when I least expected.

Not until I was trapped inside of a prison with nowhere to turn did I give serious thought to the hypocrisy of the criminal justice system. How elected officials, gavel toting magistrates, and hired wardens have never felt firsthand the effects of isolation, yet prescribe prison as a remedy? Prison has never cured poverty or crime. Crime wasn't cured through prison. Poverty didn't magically disappear as a result of shackling millions. Prison increases the likelihood of returning to these walls, making it more of a reality. Once returned, there were cold-hearted matadors full of hatred waiting. It's funny that the same matador who felt the need to tell me he didn't want me in '*his jail*' needed a bed himself, for he was later accused of sexual assault against a female coworker.

America's refusal to compassionately open its arms to those obviously struggling has become the criterion for the criminal justice system. For those starving and addicted, we have been duped into believing the one and only answer was prison. In turn, the cruelty partnered with cold cuffs and confinement has lost its chill. Prison has become common. They were shackling our children until they grow into resentful, underachieving adults. The family of those imprisoned were taught to accept prison as second nature for America, and its beloved citizens were schooled to be tough on crime and protect what they cannot even claim as their own. In a chase for what they described as sweet liberty, we brushed to the side the greatest fight of our lives; the fight against the return to slavery. A reminder of this truth was Toni Morrison's novel, '*Beloved*'.

"The mother, Seth owned a clutching fear of her child being turned over to the devilish hands of oppression, which she had managed to escape from. Seth

preferred to take the life of her beautiful daughter, rather than allow her to be destroyed by slavery and its rooted hatred."

Similarly, Nat Turner's mother murdered each of his other siblings under the context of them never having to suffer as slaves. So where does the thought of prison arise? The creator of today's carceral punishment was none other than yesterday's slave owners. Be it a fact or fiction, the truth of it all tugs at one's heartstrings. The pain of it all was nevertheless absolute. How many Seth's do you know?

Certainly mothers and father's need not go to such extremes of harming our young, but educating them can save their lives. Fight for our children, heighten the standard, and teach our children that the proper function was to live, not to exist. In doing so, we give our children a new life. America was mentally damaged. The expectation of prison, gangs, and the graveyard must be replaced by the prospect of college, climbing the corporate ladder, and celebrating life. The system, in its entirety, from daycare to our homes, to the judicial system, was broken. All by design. Pay attention people!

****

The month of December was the least bit memorable. While our families were piecing together their yearly savings, with their minds wrapped in consumption, they became one step deeper in debt, and we on this side continued to sit in prison. No Christmas trees and no halls lined with balls of jolly, only prison. Most of us ran to and from the phones trying to claw a penny or two from a loved one before the materialistic fever caught hold and monies were spent on frivolities instead of an incarcerated brother or sister. We had done this to ourselves, so we couldn't fault the justifiable thought to leave one on stuck.

The holiday season was one filled with reminisces. Though one's spirit was best to be held high, one couldn't help but think of all he had, and all he had lost. Do we dream of a white Christmas or wish for crystal snowflakes, and snowmen? No! All we dreamt of was freedom. I wonder how the free world would look if it was wrapped nice and neat and tucked underneath a tree.

"Lockdown! Lockdown!"

In a hurry everyone went rushing to their windows to see what was going down. From a distance, officers could be spotted running back and forth, to and from A-building, B-building, and C-building like headless chickens. One didn't need to see what was happening to know it was going down. Their eighty hours of physical training hadn't prepared them for this.

Simultaneously the '*Deuces*' (panic button) were being sounded. A violent eruption like that of a volcano was taking place. Prisoners were falling one after the other like the domino effect. A few hours prior, BET and MTV were plastered on the TV screens and prisoners sat glued to the tube. The new year was right around the corner. All eyes followed the countdown of the year's most popular tunes and videos. The year 2011 was coming to a close with a bang, literally. Two rival gangs had grown tired of sharing the same space and somebody had to go.

Miles beyond fist to cuffs, penitentiary knives began swinging. USP Pollock was no longer big enough. Ever so often there arose the need for downsizing. We co-exist as we intentionally ignore many things that, had we been in other areas, we would not dismiss. Then, territorial thoughts take charge and life meets death. Instantaneously the scent of blood filled the air. Isolated incidents get bloody and group demonstrations get messy. The guards knew it. Even from a respectable distance, fear could be detected in their eyes.

The C.O.'s sprinted across the compound one after the other. When violence of this magnitude breaks out, every face becomes a target, and silence means danger.

After about an hour or so, the units were covered in blood, and prisoners were dragged to the SHU while C.O.'s disappeared to shower off tear gas. My cellmate and I, along with the remainder of the prison population, were locked in our cells and left to deal with the backlash. C.O.'s normally took these types of things out on those left behind, whether they were involved or not. To make a C.O. work was to invite a bunch of bullshit. If the slogan '*how you bring in the new year is how you would spend the new year*' held any truth, I was in for a long ride.

"So what now cellie?" I asked.

"Nothing. Absolutely nothing. We sit and apply our best selves and never allow the people to see that this shit is getting to us," he responded. How being locked behind a door for extended periods of time was to be taken in stride, I had no clue, but this was all part of the '*us versus them*' mentality.

"You think they'd know by now that locking men in a cage for years and years did more harm than healing," I stated.

As if already knowing the answer, my cellie responded with rapid speed. "Yeah, they know, but pain and suffering still have to be endured with our heads held high. The basement, the roof, doors open or closed, its all prison. How you conduct yourself is what truly matters. Crying over a system that has been broken since the beginning changes nothing."

"True, but it ain't about crying, and it ain't about holding our heads high. In my book, there's no other option. The real question is, how do we change this shit?" The conversation was getting heated. Not that either of us was taking sides, but the pain of prison sometimes came out in simple discussions.

"I don't think it can be changed on our side alone. What we need is the outside world. We need a voice. We need for people to see us with compassion and not with the wrong glasses. We need the world to see us as humans. When we have this, then things will change, and not a day before."

"And what do 'we' do?" I questioned.

He answered automatically. "Show the world that this system is not one that benefits humanity, but one that further destroys it."

"Damn, bro. That's deep!"

"Yeah, but more importantly, it's real. Just make sure in the meantime and between time that it ain't your blood out there staining the concrete. Now take your ass to sleep. This the only time a man gets to rest in this joint."

With a light chuckle, I leaned back. "Aight, in the a.m."

My cellie was 5'11, a Sunni Muslim with a big beard and was in the pen for security reasons. One did not often cell with outside affiliates, but being we both were from Jersey, we got along just fine. Despite him being Muslim and my being Blood, what he had shared with me was definitely real. When looking out at the violence I was faced with daily, including the violence of today, I had to ask myself what was the sole motivator?

Taking a careful look at history, it was clear that violence didn't begin in the ghetto. It didn't begin with black faces and it didn't begin as a result of lenient gun laws. While violence was at an all-time high in urban society, we must acknowledge that poverty was its cause, not black skin. Maybe this violence started with the lynchings, the whippings, the endless cycle of abuse waged by way of slavery and the inferiority complex slave owners attempted to whip into their slaves. Maybe it started with America's conquering of natives on this very land. Maybe it started with Europe's invasion of Africa?

What I did know was that it didn't start with the two million people being held in U.S. jails. So why was it that President Obama, Vice President Biden, and their colleagues wished for the bottom half to quietly suck our thumbs, while they patted our heads with sentence reform for non-violent offenders, pretending as though this was the magical key that would unlock the doors and put an end to mass incarceration? I most certainly agreed with the sentence reform for drug offenders, but I was left to question if one does not give rise to the other. Both drugs and violence were products sponsored by the very people who imprison us. Let us take a look. Was it not President Obama who made this statement?

"They (black folks) understand that some of the violence that takes place in the poor black neighborhoods around the country is born out of a very violent past in this country, and that the poverty and dysfunction that we see in those communities can be traced to a very difficult history." -Obama, July 19, 2013

Must we pretend that this very difficult history Obama was speaking of was not the lynchings and slavery?

Pretend. Pretend. Pretend.

Instead, they want to blame it on gangbanging, gangsta rap, rated 'R' movies and graphic video games. Then again, calling a spade a spade was treasonous; the truth unimportant. This degree of violence could only be about little black boys donning hoodies, sagging pants, and colored bandannas. Starving families was a result of their own doing as babies have babies, and little boys grow too lazy to work. The defamation of black skin continues as the system offered excuses to assassinate. Furthermore, noise was made about the corner boy or the self-professed kingpin of Absentville, and not on the Americans who provided what was being sold. This was yet another avenue to destroy the bottom half.

When the guns, drugs, and violence that were force-fed into urban neighborhoods began spilling into suburban America, we were met with slogans and campaigns such as *'war on drugs'*, and were told to *'take a bite out of crime'*. Now we had a problem. The threatening of

America's upper class called for crime stoppers to pull out all the stops, but prior to little Timmy listening to Jeezy's trap music, and little Tommy twisting his fingers, nobody needed a war. Who exactly was America waging war against?

After nearly thirty days on lockdown, a cell search, the destruction of property, and countless bag meals, I was standing at my door's window around midday and watched as two officers approached my cell.

"Butler?" they asked.

"Yeah, what's up?"

"Pack up whatever property you have and have it done in 10 minutes," the officer demanded. He didn't give me any clue as to what was going on, where I was headed, or what was the need for the immediate pack up. Was I headed to the hole? Was it a court trip? I tapped on my door in demand of an answer.

Tap! Tap! Tap! Tap! Tap! Tap!

"Where I'm going?"

Curiosity was getting the best of me. I wanted to know where they were taking me. Uniformed officers had proven on many occasions that they weren't to be trusted, so taking this packout at face value was just something I couldn't do.

"You'll find out when you get there," he said with hostility in his tone.

Exhibiting correct behavior while correcting the behavior of others was too much to ask. Relaxed dialogue between officers and prisoners nearly never occurred. There had always been a superior disposition exuded on their part. Maybe this was what they were taught in training, but I'd always felt that a little bit of respect could go a long way. Was it not their job to assist inmates or was everything to be hostile? So often the smallest things caused the deadliest explosions. Men were locked up with years of frustration pinned up inside, and officer after officer wanted nothing but trouble. The unnecessary aggression displayed was oftentimes too much to shoulder. Pick at an open wound long enough, and it was bound to bleed.

Knowing that any hint of defiance on my behalf was what they wished for, I went ahead and began packing what little property I had while conversing with my cellmate. Frustration and anger walking together within me, I told my cellmate he could have everything. I tucked away my legal work, some hygiene, a pair of shoes, family photos, and readied myself to depart.

"Cuff up!" the officers commanded. After my cellie and I complied, they opened the door and took away my property, leaving me standing in the cell as they secured the door. Now I was really stumped.

"What the fuck?!" I shouted.

My cellie reading the uneasiness in my tone, sat back, and spoke. "Worry only about what you can control."

I couldn't deny the logic in his statement, yet my emotions were running high, and being rational was but a fleeting thought. There were moments like this when the cuffs locked on your wrists became tighter and a squeeze of the system manifested like a python grip. It was also when the longing for home intensified. Nothing was more bitter than prison. Where would I go from here was beyond my view. Closer to home? I seriously doubted that.

From what I'd come to know the system in large part was relentless when it came to breaking bonds and destroying the family structure. Me getting anywhere close enough to hug my son or kiss my daughter was seemingly unrealistic. All I could do was wait it out. I was looking at every step of this journey as if I was getting one step closer to freedom. The glass was half full. Thoughts of home would keep me going. I needed freedom like I needed air. Only freedom would awaken me from the grave, and when I did get free, I knew this, *"The only way to deal with an unfree world was to become so absolutely free that my very existence became an act of rebellion."* -Albert Camus.

"Butler, let's go!"

Hours later a different set of officers yelled instructions from the opposite side of my door. The clock read 11:47pm. With midnight only minutes away, the time was now. The Super Bowl had just ended with the New York Giants beating the New England Patriots. Ready to deal, I stepped out of my cell, took one look back at my cellie, and entered another section of the lion's den.

After about twenty minutes or so, I found myself with a horde of inmates inside the prisons R&D. Amongst the pack there was plenty of gossip, but not a single soul knew for sure what was taking place. The feeling read that of the middle passage, smuggled in the center of the night. Time would be the teller of what was ahead. However, no matter how extraordinary our imaginings got, we concluded that the nearest destination was USP Beaumont.

Beaumont held a similar reputation as that of Pollock. 'Bloody Beaumont' was its alias. The stories that accompanied Beaumont placed fear on the faces of many. USP Beaumont had been shut down back in 2008 after the Bureau of Prisons deemed the institution too dangerous. The body count was unbelievable. Summing it all up, the prison's closing was the result of too much bloodshed.

Now that Beaumont was reopening, we were amongst the first to fill its beds. The FBOP allowing beds to go to waste was unheard of. Besides, with the United States having the highest incarceration rate to date, every bed was already accounted for. Paint over the blood and start anew. Abandoning an entire prison for good, no way! In this gathering of men, I was sure there were many in the crowd who wondered if anyone in this room would be the first to kick off a new body count. The whole lot would never survive the dangers of prison. Either one would be sent to protective custody or one would have to enact an extreme act of violence to stake their hold and never be heard from again. Lord knows whose praying for the lost souls.

Chances were, with the opening of any prison, the likelihood of violence would skyrocket straight to Jupiter. *'Houston, we have a problem!'* Everybody had plans of laying claim to everything and there was never much of anything to be shared. The breakdown of nothing was nothing, but the prison blinders kept prisoners foolishly fighting, attempting to possess what would always be the system's.

The idiocy of it all didn't stop men from holding Mexican standoffs. When the doors opened and we were free, we would take none of the prison home with us to share with our loved ones, but who cared? Like toddlers, men grabbed hold of televisions, chairs, tables, and cells, and refused to let go. They were too busy screaming, "Mines! Mines! Mines!" This was similar to the downtrodden streets of urban America. The same ignorance we ate up, fed, and regurgitated back onto our city streets. We were warring over corners and blocks, recklessly aiming and killing kids, bringing grief to mothers, and shackling ourselves. All over the same thing: nothing.

Chapter 6

BLOODY BEAUMONT

On the bus ride to Beaumont I was humbled as I sat beside and conversed for the first time with one of my trusted comrades and co-defendants, Preston 'Death' Jones. Death was one of the solids; one of the few who felt an obligation to stand up. In fact, of us all, Death was the only one who proceeded to trial. Though he lost, he never wavered or forfeited his integrity, and held it down. If Jay-Z's slogan, '*less is more*' was actual fact, death would certainly be one of the more.

Riding in the night's darkest hours, Death and I spoke of many things. While on the streets, we had seldom spent a moment together as he was caught up doing what he needed to survive, and I was doing the same. As we rode, what we did know of one another, we spoke on. The good times, the errors in judgment, all the way down to the night he got put on the set. We even spoke of his family's dislike of me.

"But why?" I asked, more troubled by this revelation than he would ever know.

Though Death evaded my inquiry, in my heart, I knew what it was about. I'd heard it all before. If I took nothing from my sentencing day, I took the words of Magistrate Hayden, *"Every one of the talents that you have can be used over the next couple of decades. Every one of the hopes and dreams that you had can in fact be transformed into something a lot less glamorous. You have the gift of leadership, but you have used it badly."*

Maybe the hurt and anger of my loved ones and my peer's loved ones were a burden I had to carry. What troubled me was that amidst the influence, the old me felt there was nothing wrong with my '*advice*' or my '*leadership*'. There were still many who believed that everyone's fall was the result of my backward teaching. Living with this was the most difficult thing I'd ever had to deal with. Yesterday I didn't feel I was wrong in pointing out a means to survive. However, today I knew there was wrongdoing in my failure to provide alternatives like hard work, employment, and school; the application of one's best self.

America's massacre and mass incarceration were both indubitably the result of the lack of these alternatives; but wasn't it easier to blame me? Why not blame the United States for not standing solidly alongside its creation and making a change. It took pride in its astronomical incarceration rates (United States vs. Defendant). This goes to show that making it out of the ghetto didn't necessarily take for one to slang his way out or for one to be ready to kill in the event someone attempted to remove food from their plate.

I was also told that I was being too hard on myself; that the government's role was far more detrimental than my five minutes of fame. Don't we already know the government's acceptance of responsibility will never come? How long have we been waiting? We have to know that change would only come by way of our own doing.

For this, I accepted Death's family disappointment or anyone's anger with me. Who better to teach and to educate than our own? I taught what I knew, yet I knew nothing. Not because I was dumb, deaf, and blind, but because I was feeding to my people exactly what the *'people'* wished for me to teach. It was the perfect way for them to destroy us and ours. So in life's string of events, regardless of who taught me what I knew or didn't know, I played a role in the demise of dozens of men.

Realizing this, I found it a bit difficult to stare Death in his eyes. Actually, I found the darkness of the bus ride to be a bit soothing. I had made a habit of hurting those I loved the most. Prison or the graveyard, the images were always there. They lived somewhere far off in my mind. We were all just kids (mentally), and now we were to spend every year of our adult lives as imprisoned men. The one cherishing moment of the entire bus ride was when Death assured me in his quieted way that he loved me and he didn't feel a hint of resentment towards me or my leadership.

Finally, we made it, and as confused as I was, I could not have been more pleased. There was no use in prolonging the inevitable. It was time! Fresh out of the frying pan and into the fire! As we exited the bus, the oppressive conditions were illustrated on the faces of the sneering officers. The cold-hearted stares were meant to intimidate and show disgust. I leaned more toward the latter.

Once inside Receiving & Discharge, we were switched and swapped, removed from one area into another. Round and round we went, mere objects. Every single movement was a reminder that at no point were we free. The concept of shackling, stripping, and forcing us to sit idly for hours, was the highest of hurdles designed to play with a man's mind. It was created to force concession, yet the strong didn't crumble!

"There are only 2 positions behind these walls in America's prison system: victimizer or victim." -Lauryn Hill

After hours of being processed, our bedrolls were finally distributed along with paper identification cards. These paper I.D.'s came with our registration number, housing block, and photo. I had been sent off to building 1, unit A. Making my way down the compound, I knew with so much of America in chains the chances of me spotting someone with a familiar face was high. Be it a neighbor, an old little league teammate, the local dope boy or even the honor roll student who grew up following all the rules and kept his head in the books. Unfortunately, life would award the awful realization that all A's on a report card didn't exempt one from the long arms of the law.

However, a recognized face didn't guarantee refuge. With that in mind, I sought to escape the attention of those around me and discreetly wrapped the bedroll around my left arm, freeing my right. Wrapping my arm with my bedroll was a veteran move passed on by elder convicts. The bedroll wrapped around my arm would assist me in cushioning any oncoming blow, while my free hand was open to let loose in retaliation.

Upon entering the unit, I saw that everyone was all over the place. Quickly, the ring of convicts began to make hurried assessments of who was who and what was what. I too did my due diligence. The rule was to spot the movements of inmates headed in one's direction or toward their cells to arm themselves. People have had squares pushed into their bodies courtesy of shower rods.

The onslaught of prisoners with their lists of questions came next.

"Where you from?"

"What prison you came from?

"Who you run with?"

Everyone on the inside knew that everyone was not allowed to walk everywhere. Rival gangs held on sight laws and no one from a rival gang would be able to last a minute on a yard previously dominated by another. Inmates were led to cells immediately by groups of affiliates and stripped naked as they searched for enemy affiliated tattoos. The wrong branding and one may never leave that cell alive.

There were no reservations as the brutal nature of prison was run by those thirsty for blood. However, living it and seeing it on MSNBC called for a different courage and strength. Explicit warnings didn't help. Those who were scared of the dark never made it to the light. This darkness and light could possibly be viewed as heaven and hell, yet it was not relegated to prison violence alone.

Being afraid of the dark could be ascribed to one who had given up on freedom, refused to study his criminal case, indulged in every prison activity, from sports to drinking hooch, but never entered the prison library. They were too concerned with dice games, poker tables, homosexuals, and bootleg liquor. The darkness could be the one on the streets who justified his fear of living righteously, claiming he had to submit his truest self to a criminal lifestyle or he and his family would starve.

We had to do away with these well-formed excuses justifying our hopelessness and fear. Even roses have thorns. We must dare to succeed, believing victory was our right to claim. Prison, even when faced with a life sentence, doesn't mean we have to give up. Economic strife doesn't mean we have to rob, steal, and kill to put food on the table. Night comes, but it passes. We must fight because once we fell into darkness, it becomes extremely exhausting to reclaim the light.

The act of giving up came easy. Think of our sons, daughters, wives, sisters, brothers, mothers, and fathers. How do we call home stressing for fifteen minutes that they remain strong when we have fallen weak? Punishment must not suppress a man's will to survive. What it took to secure light amidst the struggle was not found in empty slogans of '*do your time*'. Many had walked through these prison doors with expectations of new beginnings, and have woken in infirmaries or died of multiple stab wounds. The danger, pain, ills of prison life, or life on the outs, was indeed real. Covering our eyes and pretending what was before us would somehow miraculously disappear was only placing us further into darkness and pushing us farther away from the light. However, no matter how dark or far off the light appeared, fear and hopelessness were not the answer.

Fearing the dark was not abnormal, but refusing to fight was cowardice!

In federal prison, arriving somewhere new was to be expected. The BOP didn't hesitate in shipping us from one prison to the next. Some switched penitentiaries like socks. The likelihood of serving your entire sentence in one spot was highly unlikely. For me, this was my fifth federal prison in ten years, notwithstanding New Jersey state prison. Hitting the yard now, all I wanted was to mellow out and pursue this new beginning. Taking into account the worst, which I couldn't let go off. Now a veteran to the code of convicts, both quiet and loud rumblings translated like a second language.

From one spot to the next, you would begin to pick up different means of survival. Things like ways to cook with the bare minimum by mixing noodles, leftovers, mayonnaise and vegetables. You will learn to sharpen flat pieces of metal against the concrete until they became razor-sharp to use as weapons. Then there were the small but very important lessons, like minding your own business. *"The best line of business was nobodies business."* This I'd been told years ago. Come what may, surviving was the first rule of thumb.

My plan to walk light enough to piss the ground off was just a plan, and plans seldom went accordingly. Indulging in prison politics was a sure way to get jammed up with other inmates or staff. So I had to breathe easy or be further suffocated. Too much time spent in the box had already set me back eons. My race to freedom was becoming longer than Mandela's, and day after day was proving to come with countless hurdles. My resilience was being tested in every direction.

"In everyone's life there comes a time of ultimate challenge. A time when all our resources are tested. A time when life seems unfair. A time when our faith, our values, our patience, our compassion, and our ability to persist are all pushed to the limit and beyond. Some have used such tests as opportunities for growth and others have turned away and allowed these experiences to destroy their hopes."

How bad did I want a new beginning? Was I standing in my own way by not attempting something different? To change the course I needed to rearrange the course of my ending. I spoke of new beginnings while failing to 'tie my camel.' I was under the impression I could speak it into existence, instead of willing it to be. What from my past did I still need? Certainly, my past made me the man I was today. I was a man with many flaws, but weren't we all? There was no need for me to hide from the mistakes within my make up. I didn't need to change my past in order to liberate myself from it. However, this was easier said than done when the penitentiary's idle time made playing in the devil's lair unavoidable. But who was looking for easy? I knew that if I could find the right path in changing my thought process, I could win.

"The secret to change is to focus all of your energy not on fighting the old, but on building the new." -Socrates

Knowledge, supported by action, would provide proof of my desire to change. So while here in Beaumont, I had to put a stop to the system's design to cuff my potential. My conditions couldn't control my cognitive thoughts and choices. That which was outside of my power was to have a limited effect on my right and wrongs. It was not always fair, yet a deck stacked against us was reality. The expectation of '*fair*' simply because one had made the decision to change was foolish. The greater the belief, the greater the struggle.

Mere months after I'd touched the yard, the prison's Special Investigations Specialist called me to the L.T.'s office, professing to have received reports that I had begun '*squeezing*' inmates, I could do nothing but laugh. Change in itself was the challenge. Now that I was attempting to shift my negatives into positives, I had to be expectant of suspicion. My battle to regain my freedom meant I would have to battle to change their perception. Thus, my change could not be about them. What I needed was to break free from my own wayward beliefs. For now, I had to war against the administration in an attempt to free myself from their unfounded allegations.

After thirty minutes of being unreceptive to their stated intent to lock me up, if they received one more complaint, I grabbed my belongings and went back to my unit to face my frenemies. Frustration could be seen in my walk as I carried a heavy mind. The weight of the similarities between the prison administration and our criminal justice system was ridiculous. Both having the ability to handicap a man's life on nothing more than hearsay was simply asinine.

Actual guilt meant zero in the distribution of justice. Disregard the fact that the deck would always be stacked against certain individuals. The system still went above and beyond to makeshift the burden of proof. Whatever a man had done yesterday was what the world believed he was after today. That was enough substantial evidence to support the pointed finger. They didn't give us a chance to change. The fact that man could wake up every day, and fight the constant oppression delivered in prison, was him attempting to give himself a chance. But who cared?

There were many who refused to go on. Daily you see men being held accountable for one another's mistakes, the punishment at times two-fold. When his power or influence pulled for positive, it was often brushed aside as an expected course of action. The only chance we were given was to serve hard time. The marginalized theory of our criminal justice system as the solution to fix society was largely responsible for a man's reluctance to '*buy-in*'. You didn't hear this from me.

Here in prison there was not a single incentive. Not a single reason encouraging men toward positive change. A man serving eighty-five percent of his sentence had no room for relief. Instead, he had fifteen percent left to be chewed upon like hungry hyenas ripping through the flesh of a lion. There were a few programs to assist in the rehabilitation process. However, there was always that fine print that states you must have three to five years remaining on your sentence, and violent offenders were not to receive the same benefits as those with nonviolent crimes. Violent offenders and life sentence serving inmates were to sit and rot, yet play nice in the sandbox.

With this truth, the administration's threats proved to be non-consequential for a majority of the prison population. They could not take any more than they had already taken from us when they sentenced us to sit still. So as the prison system raged with violence, the question became: Who were the real perpetrators? Would it be those committing the violence on the outside or those igniting it by decimating hope?

****

Despite the threats of the administration and the plots of inmates to get me out the way by running to tell Massa, I continued to walk. Yet, what was I walking towards? Freedom! In this same penitentiary I'd taken the steps to secure my Associate Degree in Psychology through correspondence with Ashworth College. I took every program the prison had to offer that didn't preclude me and managed to stay incident-free. My mind was fixated on freedom and survival. Through this model behavior they never noticed my '*walk*'. They were too busy running in and out of my cell trying to trap me and coming up with nothing. Something had to give.

The administration seemed to have it out for me and returning me to the box became more likely every single day. All the right buttons were being pushed, yet, I refused to bite the bait. I didn't respond like '*Massacre*' and this drove them crazy. The man or animal they thought I was, or read about in pre-sentence reports and confidential documents from other institutions, wasn't adding up. Something was wrong, but what was it?

Though they were clueless, it was my truth. A truth which said I was growing inwardly stronger in a place that was known to curtail man's mind, body, and soul. I was combating their repressive maneuvering with something akin to Dr. Cornel West's '*Black Prophetic Fire*'. I held an inextinguishable urgency to overcome my circumstances on my own terms or I would die trying.

As time wore on, they continued to hit my cell trying to put away my fire. Sometimes they would go as deep as the ocean with their attempts. I knew they could smell the stench of smoke rising from my every action. In their opinion, where there was smoke there was sure as hell fire. They would chase behind my phone calls, my emails, and my snail mail. The scrutiny was identical to what I remembered myself going through when the Feds were secretly investigating me and my gang for Federal Racketeering. After continued failed attempts, they decided to hit me where it hurt.

Having gone years without physical contact with the free world, anticipation woke me earlier than usual. It was early, yet the cell was still dark. I didn't want to wake my cellmate, so I quietly picked through my khaki uniforms, cologne, underclothes, and boots. As soon as the doors opened I was heading to the shower, preparing myself for the dance floor.

The sight of the visiting hall remained vivid in my mind. I remember the miscellaneous things such as the rows of chairs and the tables which separated visitors from the visited. The snack machines were equipped with all sorts of things allowing couples to get vending machine wasted. There would be little kids laughing, others crying. There were sounds of whispered words exchanged by loved ones trying their best not to be heard by those within earshot; all of it remained music to my ears. A tune that could not be heard, nor carried when prisoners were ordered to head back. Prisoners were sent one way while visitors were sent another.

What this tune brought to mind for me was family, love, and connectedness. Every man here longed for this temporary harmony. This was not a feeling held by me alone, but by the masses of incarcerated men and women. The 2.3 million people chained, all dreaming the most beautiful dreams. Dreams of again having the ability to be as close as prison would allow. In the visiting hall, everyone's emotions were the same; race and gender meant nothing. I could not wait for this quick reprieve from the everyday punishments of prison. This visit would reawaken in me something that I felt had died a long time ago.

Not soon after my morning shower, I stood standing in my cell putting the final touches on my visiting attire when out of the blue my cell door swung open. Standing in the entranceway was the unit officer.

"Butler!" the C.O. shouted.

Thinking this was my call to visit, I hurried my response while grabbing my khaki shirt.

"Yeah," I shot back.

"They want you at the L.T.'s office."

The look on my face quickly shifted from one of elation to dismay. From the time mentioned, until this very moment, I had seen the L.T.'s office only once. For me or any prisoner for that matter, who was not checking into protective custody or secretly offering up information, a trip to the L.T.'s office was like a trip to the courthouse. Nothing good ever came of it. Not sure what I had done, I tried my best to speed up the process, believing this was either a mishap or a minor infraction that wouldn't warrant a trip to the hole. As I headed down the compound, confused and trying to conceal the puzzled look on my face, I ran into about five of my Blood homies, all asking where I was headed.

"The L.T.'s office. One of ya'll come up there with me real quick," I said, after remembering the penitentiary laws with respect to never conversing with staff without another convict present.

Agreeing to accompany me was the L-Gang homie, Ryder out of New York City. While taking off, the homie Boodah from '*Beven Nine Trey*' out of Newark, New Jersey asked me if I thought everything was good, since he and I both were anticipating visits. We had known one another prior to the cuffs being slapped on.

Once inside the L.T.'s office, the Captain aggressively told Ryder to leave unless he planned on going with me. The Captain's assertiveness immediately raised antennas. Something was brewing. Collectively, like the falls of Niagara, the L.T. and Captain began raining on me with accusations and threats. I felt like I was a child in school being bullied by the so-called cool kids. What I had or hadn't done was obsolete at this point. A point needed to be made, and I was the example. In their minds, they were the ruling force, and at their mercy was where I belonged. There was no justifying insubordination. Trying to make sense of bucking the system that they contributed their dollars to, meant someone had to pay the price.

"So you think its funny our officer has been killed?" yelled the Captain.

The confusion on my face couldn't be concealed. I smirked as I responded, thinking this was a certified claptrap. "What?!"

Staring through squinted eyes, the L.T. and I faced off. His aggression serving as a weapon to provoke me. Calmly, I listened as both the L.T. and the Captain began reading a post I had written on a collaborative blog site created by Kamaal Bennett and myself titled '*Live From Lockdown*'. Their interpretation of my post was that I was an unsympathetic asshole who was condoning violence against officers. This was similar to what the government had done to me in 2002 when they forwarded the History Channel's series "Gangland" excerpts of what was actually said to paint a vicious visual of my person and agenda.

The L.T. continued reading, bouncing around sentences as though for sport. I tried to interrupt on occasion, but to no avail.

"If you keep reading you will see all of what I said," I protested, but reading the entire post was to admit that I was right. Let's not forget that I was a prisoner, and prisoners were to be nothing more than weak, and once again, '*might was right*'.

"Butler, you're going to the hole."

"For what?" I asked again.

Though the post may seem uncompassionate, the truth of the matter was, it was no infraction other than having unremorseful feelings towards an officer who had taken a hit. This happened daily to inmates, and the most you will get from an officer was a blank face and the command, *"Clean up the blood and keep it moving."* They were taught not to feel for us. As a result of their callousness, there became a greater line of separation where both sides lacked empathy towards each other. Somehow, to voice this truth was something I had to be locked up for. Refusing to let me *'win'*, my superiors had concocted a frivolous excuse to lock me down.

"Other officers may not agree with your statements and may want to retaliate, so we have to lock you up for your safety," said the L.T.

Again, I laughed, understanding that this was all a big show. Mentally, I pondered how long they would continue to get away with these sorts of injustices, speaking of retaliation by other officers in the form of violence, when they themselves were being retaliatory in sending me to the hole. Dressing it up as though locking me up was for my physical safety. Their design was to mentally, and emotionally cripple me by leaving me in the hole for an undetermined period of time. The instruction was for officers to not *'feel'* in order to maintain a level of professionalism. Then you tell me there was a good chance these same officers wouldn't be able to honor professionalism, so I needed to be detained. What were we to believe of justice?

"If the goal of justice is not simply revenge, we must have a route to amelioration in mind every step of the way." -Maya Schenwar

The truth is, those who believe in justice were color blind and wanted the best for all races, and creeds. Today we were faced with the reality of our criminal justice system being full of individuals motivated by hatred, biases, racist ideas, and flat out vengeance.

Following the ill-thought-out excuses to send me to the hole, I was thrown in the holding tank and left to wait until officers could escort me to the hole. While waiting, I sat in the center of the tank's freezing air. I was dressed in the same khaki uniform I thought I would be wearing for my visit. I had to deal with different staff members walking by and mocking my predicament as an added means of intimidation. Internally, I was both pissed and humored by the games of *'professionals'*.

Further frustrating me was the idea of my visitor standing in line outside being subjected to physical scrutiny with absolutely no clue as to my current situation. At any minute she would be turned away with no reasoning and the miles she'd traveled would be irrelevant. A barrage of harassing thoughts played in my mind. Images of the hundreds of miles visitors traveled all for nothing whenever a visit was terminated at the last minute. A family enthusiastically trekking down the interstate just for a hug and a glimpse into the eyes of their loved one.

Plaguing my mind were visions of the punishment my family confronted as a result of my not being free. Sights of the financial strains and how a canceled visit could symbolize months of rent wasted, food removed from the dinner table or possibly the destruction of any dream forever shared between two lovers stood out in my mind. This unjustified chaining would certainly serve as a means to crush the spirits of my support system. I wondered what a prisoner being in the hole meant for families who waited for hours in line to visit one they rarely touched and seldom saw. Would my visitor believe me to be selfish? Would we be able to recover?

"Tewhan, how could you get in trouble, knowing I was coming to visit?"

I could already hear the clear pain in her voice. The system's spiteful ways were making me out to be a liar to my loved one. Family members hearing me tell them how good I was doing would wonder how I ended up in the hole. With the hole constricting me to letters and once a month phone calls, it would take days for me to explain a situation that still didn't make sense to me. How do you make sense of going to the hole for drawing parallels between one instance and another? With no incident report I was being held under investigation, awaiting clearance from the Counter-Terrorist Division, or so I was told. Instead of jotting down their lies and mailing it home, I opted for the truth.

"I'm in the hole right now as a result of their fear of my voice and people listening." A fearless voice reaching a concerned people was a dreaded reality they did not want to face. Clearly put, I was locked up because I was not quiet.

After writing this letter I still couldn't expect my family to understand fully. Why would they not be fooled when most of

America was shamed every day believing those we have entrusted with power do not abuse it? With the same manipulating skills politicians use to advance the building of innumerable prisons, the system awards retaliatory punishments behind these walls. Some identical to that of Guantanamo Bay.

The free world society paid attention to the cover, but never considered the crushing content. This trickery caused American's to expect the worst of everyone, even its own; believing the top one percent to not only be right, but mighty. Our very own families having trouble tilting in our favor when we were being weighed by the scales of justice. Not even my cellmate, Johnny 'Crusher' Jackson, believed I could be locked up for something so farfetched, while he himself was in the hole under another one of USP Beaumont's strings of investigations.

During this period, at least seventy-five percent of Beaumont's hole population was filled with prisoners under investigation. Most resulting in nothing, other than a way to bleed men in isolation for undetermined periods without necessarily violating policy. These investigations were nothing but waiting games. Not a single staff member was telling me anything and my pride prevented me from asking. My pride wanted the administration to see me accepting their punishment with a smile on my face rather than shedding a tear. My ego was defending itself and so I took their unjustified punishment and made it my business to laugh whenever they made their weekly rounds into the Special Housing Unit.

On far too many occasions I had witnessed inmates being labeled as '*bitches*' by staff for asking questions as harmless as, '*When am I being released from SHU?*' This was the staff's way of applying reverse psychology to deter inmates from pursuing the justice they were entitled to. Looking back I saw where many of us on the inside think with our hearts rather than our heads. We would prefer to endure injustice as opposed to fighting against the powers that be, simply because '*they*' deemed fighting as a bitch move. When, in fact, quietly sitting by and accepting injustice of any kind was to embody weakness. The '*reputation is one's wealth*' mentality was being wrongly applied and was leading to men refusing the pursuit of justice. '*Manhood over scholastics*', was what it was called.

Most men in prison had lost everything, from friends to family. Their reputations were all they had left. Having it tarnished by being labeled weak, or a coward, was something that many refused to risk despite who was doing the labeling. Ignorance has taught men to demand respect via the convict code and leave them drowning at sea without a safety net. This ignorance was not their fault, but simply the rule of the day.

For nearly all one's life, men have been treated *as men* inside of their respective communities. This called for fistfights, shootouts, and iron men contest. When it came time to apply oneself on a larger scale and outside of the neighborhood, one was at a loss as to how to survive. The administration studied men in prison for years and knew this was a sure shot method to treat us cruelly and to utilize our own ignorance to keep us quiet about it. In prison there were grievance forms called BP-8, BP-9, up to BP-11's, where an inmate could file a complaint to superior staff. However, around ninety percent of the prison population refused to take advantage of these remedies for fear of appearing weak. My own ignorance had me stuck in the hole for thirty days with a hushed tone and a smile, believing myself to be a gangsta for it. Despite my crippled brilliance, on day thirty, the L.T. showed up at my door, mouth full of chewing tobacco, and an incident report in hand.

"Butler, you know your rights, don't you?" asked the L.T., too lazy to read them off. He was doing everything in a rush as though a paycheck wasn't what they worked for. Outside of having the right to remain silent, I never took the liberty of familiarizing myself with the remaining rights afforded to me on drafted documents written over a hundred years ago. Imagine how many were just like me, unaware of their legal rights and as a consequence, were manipulated. Not wanting to appear as foolish as I was for not knowing, I responded trying to sound confident. "Yeah, I know them."

Pleased to have a lightened workload, the L.T. slid my incident report through the side of the door and walked away. What the incident report read, I didn't know until my cellmate, Crusher, asked to see it. After reading it, he shook his head.

"Damn, Joe. They got you."

That was all I needed to hear to validate what I'd already known. The fix was in.

"What it say, bro?" I asked.

In short, the incident report read none of what I was in the hole for. The Special Investigation Specialist reported that I had been responsible for running a business from inside the institution which was prohibited and that I had been instructing people on the outside as to how to make greater financial gains. I'd been had! As if bleeding in the hole for thirty days for something I hadn't done was not enough, they took it further by stretching the truth and manipulating the report.

This was not justice, but in their eyes, my just due. Already I'd had little faith in the system. This miscarrying of justice only advanced my disbelief. The system dismissed its contribution to the broad stroke of dissension drawn daily between them and us. Each instance where we were made to prove our innocence, instead of being awarded the right to be proven guilty beyond reasonable doubt, proved freedom was not free.

Those proclaiming to value justice were being outed, and cared not as they further abused the freedomless. America on all levels systematically treated its bottom half as enemies by refusing equal rights to all, even in its most minuscule matters. The world may dismiss issues such as manipulated reports by prison authorities. As a result, the detriment to those being taken advantage of was deadly (mentally, emotionally, and physically). Any system believing a person duly convicted should be subject to slavery was wrong. So that night in the hole when I went to sleep, I wondered if it would ever end.

A few long and draining days later, I was wearing orange shorts two sizes too big, an orange t-shirt one size too small, orange shower shoes, and iron handcuffs. The L.T. escorted me into a small room within the hole to have a detention hearing. Walking to the DHO (Detention Hearing Officer), I felt as though I was approaching the gas chamber. Mentally the hearing was draining. The chances of receiving a fair opportunity of proving oneself free from any wrongdoing was more so a formality.

The moment a man entered into the DHO, their future would be determined. There wouldn't be anyone fighting for your cause. There would be only you and the system. This was often the time when one law enforcement officer took the written word of another law enforcement officer. Your argument was snubbed, guilt was found with little to no reason, and a period of confinement was handed down. During these moments of walking in and out of the DHO, it was pertinent that one walked with their head up and chest out.

'Man doesn't head to and from war with a look of fear or defeat on their face.'

Once inside the DHO, flicking through paper's was an older African American woman with salt and pepper dreadlocks. She had a look on her face that read, *'my blackness does not mean leniency or allegiance'*. How did she know I expected anything? Whiteface or Blackface, it really didn't matter. All I wanted was a fair chance. However, race relations in America had branded us mentally to the point where one could not help but see sides.

What I wanted was not a side. I didn't want leniency. I wanted understanding, truth and justice. Who better to understand what was happening to the black man than the black woman. Consequently, this was the system, and similar external features didn't award me or anyone else extra favor. Though today's lopsided incarceration rate was evidence that someone, somewhere, was benefitting. But how dare I muster the thought?

Bringing me back from my thoughts was the sound of her voice.

"So, Mr. Butler, you have an incident report for misuse of email. It says here you are receiving and sending third party emails. It also says that you are running a business from inside the institution."

Just as I was ready to interject, she continued, " But what I don't understand is why they have failed to present a detailed description substantiating the infraction."

Taking this as my moment, I quickly shot back. "That's because there is none." Figuring I would get hammered anyway, I had to at least shoot that out there.

"Mr. Butler, I didn't ask you for your help. L.T. you can take him back to his cell. This hearing is postponed until I look more into this matter." A feisty undertone mounting as she spoke.

While grabbing my arm and directing me out the door, I blurted out my question.

"So am I supposed to just sit in the hole and wait?" A postponement could go on for days, weeks, even months.

"Let's go, Butler!" instructed the escorting officers.

"Hold on L.T. Butler, how much time do you have on your sentence?" asked the DHO.

Wondering what difference it made, I answered anyway. "30 years, why?"

"I just wanted to know if you had somewhere to go. Now send him back to his cell."

Once I was secured back in my cell, I couldn't help but share my thoughts with my cellmate. The entire process was for nothing and the smart ass statement at the end had me wishing I'd responded with just as much sarcasm and venom.

"Cellie, would you believe that the whole time I was sitting in there all I could see was this sister participating in the shackling of our race. All for a paycheck. A sister!"

I felt a mixture of anger and shame. Though she owed me nothing, the fact that she couldn't or wouldn't take notice of her role in the destruction of the black race was sickening. This sister's face reminded me of Angela Yvonne Davis. So why couldn't she see that prisons were obsolete? Why didn't she see that this job of hers was not a job, but an act which expanded the prison industrial complex; an industry fueled by racism; a system that was reportedly responsible for 1.5 million imprisoned black men in America.

I wondered if she participated in this symbolic lynching as a consequence of instilled self-hatred, or if this was the product of a miseducated negro. Despite my questions, I couldn't blame her. I knew if I had a home, it too would be made of glass. Many of us live hypocritical lives. Many of us have lost ourselves and our purpose. We were shellshocked, grabbing hold of self-destructive behaviors; be it gangbanging, black on black crime, or hustlers peddling crack, it was all a means to aiding and abetting a criminal justice system that enslaved us. They were all here to handicap African American communities far and wide, most times for a little bit of nothing.

Everything I was expressing to my cellmate, he was no stranger to. He had been born and raised in the gutters of one of America's most violent cities, Chicago. It was so dangerous, it had been dubbed '*Chiraq*'; home of the Gangster Disciples, Latin Kings, Black P. Stones, Vice Lords, and Obama. Raised and shaped by his conditions, as us all, there was no wonder he and I were bound and confined to the same cell. For it was the conditions more than the people that paved the way for mass incarceration.

Weren't we all believers that the way of the world affected the way we as a people exist? When you take a seed, plant the seed, and desire for the seed to grow, you nurture the seed with what it needs. You don't place the seed inside a dark room with the expectancy for it to blossom to its full potential. This was the same for humans. You cannot take a person and subject them to negative environmental factors such as neighborhoods soiled with guns, drugs, and violence, and expect for its inhabitants to reach great heights. Indeed, there would be exceptions to the rule but, in most instances, nature will win out, leaving most in the dark to wither away and die.

In cities like Chicago, there were few choices. These choices were not those of which college to attend. Instead, they were plagued with which colors to wear to school, because the wrong color could get you killed. Try focusing on your math quiz when students were up and down the halls with guns tucked in their backpacks, and weed smoke filled the air of the school bathroom. Ta-Nehisi Coates spoke of kids pulling pistols outside of convenience stores and never letting off a shot.

The ghetto I knew was a place many were too afraid to enter. The only glimpse caught of these places was on the ten o'clock news. A place where, when kids pull out pistols they use them and another life was lost. One gun, two guns, three guns, Bang! The system and the graveyard. People, there was no coincidence that those who were funneled to prison were on the darker side of brown and just so happen to suffer from poverty, crime, and violence.

"*Why are so many Black men in prison?*" asked author Demico Boothe. I would sum it up with this: The black man in America has never been seen as a complete being; nothing more than property to be done away with as pleased. While we view our skin as a blessing, for most of our skin represents everything they despise.

"Butler, let's roll!"

At my door was one of the three Marshall sisters. I was being released from the SHU. The hearing officer had given me no news and so the sudden word of my release was definitely a surprise. I was being set '*free*'. There was a cheerful moment of being released from prison inside of prison, and although I was being released to another part of the jail, I still felt a sense of relief. The hole was that part of the jail where many men got lost; where dudes lose their minds and lose themselves. It was filled with blood splatters, thrown feces, screaming in the middle of the night, police beatings that were covered up, and cellmate fights.

All of this madness happened at a much higher rate than on the prison compound. Population and its privileges offer a little bit of something, while the hole awards a whole lot of nothing. As I changed out my oranges into my prison browns I felt ashamed. I realized this *'joy'* was the resort of the psychological rearranging the system had fixed on me. Had I lost my mind and myself and did not know it? How had I let freedom become so distant that I lost the potency of the connection?

My compound cell was a combination of my home (bathroom, kitchen, living room, and bedroom). I had become so wrapped up that I was calling it *'home'*. I loathed how prison was said to be a correction for the errored ways of men, when it only incapacitated a man's train of thought as opposed to redeveloping it. Still, we have millions screaming, *"Prison, Prison!"* These same callers for prison fail to realize they were calling for death to people.

"Don't come back, boy!" the tallest of the Marshall sisters spoke with a southern drawl, as the SHU sliders were opening. I had a green army property bag thrown over my shoulder, a wrinkled uniform, and a wide eye. I was on my way back to the jungle.

****

In twenty-four hours I was back on the compound and before I knew it the homies were calling my name.

"Ayo, Mass. One of your homies wants you at the back window," shouted another prisoner from inside my unit.

"Aight. Tell'em I said hold up!"

My peace was instantly disturbed despite my already upset mental state. When the homies called, you answered, and so to the back window I went to see what was poppin'. Surely it could've been a comrade offering salutations due to my return from solitary. However, my gut told me it was something different. Peaceful times were short-lived behind the wall. The constant drama at times made lockdowns and solitary enjoyable. Now that I was out, my peace meant nothing. Something was in the air soon to spill over. If prison taught me anything, it made me certain that what was in the dark would, sooner or later, come to the light.

In this particular instance, I was being summoned to the yard to brighten a situation where no matter what the finding, the end would be dark for someone. The self-inflicted shaping of prison-made many of the people here expectant of only slow singing and flower bringing. Here the clouds were never-ending. Righteous intent left men in positions to be baptized by fire.

It was just as I thought. After a brief conversation at the back window, and a few short days later, the deuces (emergency sirens) were sounding, blood was being shed, and I was being led back to the hole. At 9pm that night, correctional officers entered my unit and exited with me in tow. Destination, SHU C-range. In the feds no one got away with anything. Until there was someone in the box, the right man or wrong guy, the entire prison would remain locked down.

As I neared the L.T.'s office, which was now becoming a regular occurrence for me, I saw my younger comrade, Junior, from Oklahoma's Red Mob standing off to the side in cuffs, and a blazing smile on his face. He and I were to wear it all.

"Come on, yawl know the way," the younger Marshall sister spoke.

With a slight hesitation, we took to the trail. One step after the other, the emptiness of the chilling corridor leading to the hole began blaring. One would never get used to that feeling in the pit of your stomach as you found your way.

Buuuuzzzzzz! The sound of the door buzzed loudly.

"We got two," shouted the C.O. through the intercom as the door began opening and closing with a deafening thud. We both stepped inside with a pseudo-two-step as though I was not troubled by my speedy return.

"Sizes, sizes. Come on yawl, it's time for me to go home," the tallest of the Marshall sisters shouted as she rushed to change us out, cell us up, and be done with her eight hour shift. We all knew prison was no place for exaggerated feelings, yet the environment made it difficult to not twist up emotions at times.

The emotion carefully scripted behind Ms. Marshall's cold stare was one of disappointment. "You just couldn't stay out, huh?" she asked. The sass in her tone saying it all.

Of all the times I'd heard that same tone, saw that same stare, it wasn't until then that I realized a setback for one was a setback for all. If you failed to respect you and yours, the possibility of another respecting you and yours was highly unlikely. Prison made a way for men to blindly hold on to the misconception that everything one did affected only self, disregarding the entirety of those whom he was connected to. This selfish train of thought helped to dismantle us all. There was no one man or one woman. For better or worse, we were interconnected, and our lives called for one love.

We have to implement more than the same jab, jab, hook that we threw at every obstacle that came our way. Though I knew this sister from nowhere beyond these prison walls, it was true that each time she stepped inside these doors, these sneering co-workers of hers were drawing parallels between her skin and our actions. Every time a beautiful black sister raised up and declared that every black man was a king, they wouldn't hesitate to remind her and those like her that we were today moving backward as a result of brave hearts, and weak minds. Standing in front of Ms. Marshall, I tried my best to avoid eye contact. I knew no matter what words she chose, the windows of her soul held over four hundred years of pain and torture endured by us all.

As I was being led back on to C-range I couldn't help but feel a sense of shame, though I kept my head up and walked as though embarrassment was not what I was feeling. At my first steps inside, inmates began calling my name, welcoming me back. Failure had somehow become acceptable and commended. Our ability to blame the system robbed us of accountability, making everything wrong in our life someone else's fault. We question why many were not on the outs fighting for us? We had failed to begin fighting for ourselves.

Yes, there have been hunger strikes and assaults on officers, though senseless. Families have stood in front of the prison screaming, *"Let my people go!"* but a balanced brawl, utilizing our minds has not been done. This assault was much deeper than the SHU. This was about the hundred or so inmates trapped inside special housing as a result of allowing the system to beat us with mind over matter issues.

There was no secret that a lot of us came from communities with some of America's highest rates of crime. There was no mystery that African American men were sentenced to a prison term twenty to fifty times longer than white males convicted of the same drug offenses. No, it was not puzzling when the numbers showed that one in every three black males born today can expect to go to jail at some point in their life, compared to one in every seventeen white males.

These truths were assets and products to facilitate growth, not excuses to be used to justify failure. Prison doesn't have to mean death. Education systems designed to purposefully fail students doesn't mean we should run to the streets. A corner filled with crack dealers and drug addicts doesn't mean we have to be hopeless. Resilience was culminated by all things which did not bury us six feet underground. The hurdles, the barriers, and the blocks were real, yet we can overcome. We can, in due time, enjoy the fruits of our labor, but this requires hard work. Without hard work, commitment, and a desire to change what has been, the destruction of our entire race will continue to be, both in and out of prison.

****

"Get up Blood. They're doing rec," whispered Junior. With so much on my mind the night before, I couldn't account for anything beyond the stare of Ms. Marshall. On the other hand, Junior had already been up and at it. Recreation was mandatory following the morning after entering the hole. It was similar to a roll call. Missing recreation was not a good look and could easily be perceived as 'ducking rec'.

Rain, hail, sleet, or snow, ducking rec would get you branded as a coward, afraid of the unknown. So with an ashy face, breath stinking, and sweaty armpits from sleeping in my orange jumpsuit, I hopped out of bed and stood in the dark. It was 6 a.m. and we were required to be at the door suited and booted like the military.

"Ya'll going to rec?" asked a female C.O., clipboard in hand, and a wig that seriously needed help.

"Yeah, we going," Junior and I drowsily responded in unison.

"Mass, that you? What you doing back here?" she said, surprised to see me in the box.

"Yeah, it's me and for the regular. You know they weren't going to let me stay out there too long."

"Oooohhhh, okay then. I'll be right back. One of your disrespectful ass homeboys been back here acting up. Wait till I tell his punk ass you back here."

Working for the police was a serious no go. The prison population, both staff and inmates alike, knew that we held a certain code of conduct and the behavior that the homeboy was allegedly indulging in was unacceptable when it came to the homies. Still, I stood in disbelief, shaking my head because it was as if she hadn't heard a single word I'd said.

I know her intent was not to ignore my circumstances, however, this was not the time. The last thing I needed was to catch another charge while in the hole. But who cared? Nobody cried for the bad guy. In the end, as long as they weren't left with the tab, it would be all smiles and fun and games until a whispered word led to cold steel penetrating flesh, life sentences, and no one leaving. This shit was wicked and I couldn't seem to wrap my hands around the top to bottom machiavellian traits of all who touched this place. Trust me, this wasn't where you wanted to be.

The disrespectful homeboy was actually a pretend tough guy. He was checked into protective custody for fondling himself in front of female officers, and he hadn't touched the compound since. Now back in the hole, he claimed he was '*sick*', and as a result couldn't keep his hands out his pants.

Aside from him, there were the usual Bloods, Crips, G.D.'s, and neutrals from different cities and states. Junior and I had yet to receive an incident report. The bad news was that this game could go on forever. Junior had already decided he would take the charge, which meant they would be releasing me back to the compound. He had only sixty days left on his sentence and no more good time to lose.

"This shit ain't nothing blood," he stated flatly. The only problem was, to resolve the issue, we had to be seen. Once inside the box and locked behind that metal door, the staff got to you when they decided. Things like '*due process*' were figments of one's imagination. Your ass could rot forever. "*Tell it to the judge!*"

****

The penitentiary gods must have heard the prayers of the good men serving their twenty-three and one as they should. The prison had suddenly been assigned a new head sis. On day one, he made his rounds, door to door, making it clear what his first line of business was: to clean out the hole. Either you were being kicked back to the yard or you could expect an increase in your frequent flier miles courtesy of the FBOP.

Hell, what more could one ask for. When you broke the law, the law sets out to break you. Your play was to stand strong and take the consequences as they may. The evidence didn't change anything. Either the guilt was there or not. The months of *'investigative work'* were nothing less than cruel and unusual punishment.

When it came time for this new Special Investigative Specialist (SIS) to interview Junior and me, the way he handled his business had to be respected.

"Sit down! Butler, you know who I am?" he questioned, a bit of authority in his voice. Clearly this wasn't his first rodeo.

"No, I don't know who you are." I hated to crush his ego, but the truth was, I had never heard of him.

"In fact, you should. I know exactly who you are Massacre." As he spoke, he looked directly in my eyes searching for a reaction of some sort. I'd seen this movie before. The only thing that changed was the leading role. "Yeah, Mass. I know you. Just like I know your boys Mr. Tyree, Mad Dog, and Ice Bomb. I had them down in Talladega SMU."

All of the names he'd just mentioned were reputable comrades in the system who had been putting in their fair share of work throughout. But what was his angle, I wondered. The name dropping supposedly was his way of letting me know he'd been around. Still, whatever he was selling, I wasn't buying. I wanted one of two things and that was it: my walking papers or designation to my next penitentiary. When SIS made a recommendation, the powers that be listened.

"Here's the deal. My cameras didn't catch what actually happened on the yard. However, we have an inmate in the hole with two black eyes, a fractured jaw, and the look of a deer caught in the headlights. Maybe he deserved what he got, but we can't have that sort of violence on this yard. As I told you, since my cameras didn't catch you, I'm going to kick you back out."

"This is how I'm running shit from now on. Consider this cops and robbers. It's your job to beat me and it's my job to catch you. I won't put shit on you or leave you in the hole under frivolous investigations. Nonetheless, you better believe when I get you, I got you, and I don't want to hear no crying."

"Say no more," I replied in short.

He was talking my language. I had no plans of doing dirt, but I also understood that this was a prison and anything was liable to happen. When it did, I would take my lick. Until then, no one wanted to deal with officers owning petty feelings, planting contraband, and writing up minuscule infractions simply to fuck up a man's time. With that said, the SIS pointed to the door, and I was free to hit the yard yet again.

After a few weeks on ice, it was time to thaw out. How long would I stay on the yard, I had no clue. Not that I couldn't keep my nose clean, but it was more so a combination of my past and my reputation haunting me. The system had a way of accounting for every miscue, figuring you'd lay in the bed you'd made, past or present.

Another morning on the inside didn't afford redemption. My inked flesh and past of "Turn up Tuesdays" couldn't be overlooked. My yesterday's chase for instant gratification was negatively affecting my future. As a consequence, I hadn't been allowed to dream in years. As politicians made their rallying cry, *"The future of America is promising."* the question remained: Why were there countless overpacked prisons full of bodies destroyed by calloused laws stemming from their past? (Criminal history, prior convictions, and probationary terms).

Regardless of how far off in the future we dreamed, the judicial system in its entirety would continue punishing us for our past. How did I break free from the errors of my past, if I was never allowed to move forward? Life didn't come with a switch permitting you to smother yesterday. There was no escape. Truth be told, I had no reason to run from it. A man was a compilation of his errors, building upon the wrong way and making it right.

Therefore, as long as I had the power to choose, my past could not be the determining factor in my present. I possessed the ability to choose and to transform, despite the many who said I couldn't. So while I was back in population, amidst the fist fights, stabbings, and the prison politics, I had to revolutionize my 'I'. I needed to create a clearer pathway to finding myself. Understanding that I needed to do something was the first step. Formation! Forward! Then October 13th came and things changed for the worse.

****

Chapter 7

When The Levy Breaks

October 13th

The seasons were fast fading and so was hope. Everyone wanted out but couldn't find an escape. The frustrations of being trapped could be contained but for so long before, "Boom!" When things finally spilled over, there was the possibility of blood overflowing. How to release certain stress and frustration was not learned by everyone. Alternative methods of release were not known so many acted in violence.

In Bloody Beaumont, what else was there to be expected other than blood? The name definitely lived up to the hype and violence was the pedigree. As prison stripped you of all your influence and affluence; your wealth and your riches; your every action following imprisonment was one committed in an attempt to reclaim your manhood and dignity. Everything you did was done to the extreme. On this morning, day broke and so did the levy. Having grown to expect the unexpected, I was sure none of us expected to be the leading character in what quickly escalated into a horror flick.

Saturday morning, we were up and prepared for a day of college football. This ritual spanned far and wide in the prison system. Everyone was up, prepping their meals for the dayroom tailgating, microwaved fried rice, nacho bowls, and penitentiary style pizza. Prison wine was brewing, and the ticket men (jailhouse bookies), posted around the unit collecting bet after bet. No matter what aromas clouded the air, and regardless of who was doing what, death was always the most present.

"Yo, Boodah, who you like bro?" I asked, trying to get a lock for my ticket.

"Bama and the over. That's a 2pk lock!" he replied.

When it came to booking favorites in sports, Boodah was as lucky as they came, though he would swear up and down it was pure skill.

"Mass, I'm telling you, Texas tech going to run that shit up," shot my man Face from D.C.

"Nigga you don't know shit about no sports," Boodah joked with Face.

"Goddamn, Slim, you be hating like shit," Marty from D.C. interrupted while sitting at the table with another D.C. homie, Lil' Head.

Lil' Head was the youngest of us all, and besides me and Face, he had the most time with a 55 year stretch to stare down. In this unit, this was our crew. Being out in Texas, and us all coming from back north, we linked up and held things down. Ironically, not all Bloods and D.C. natives got along. It derived from a long line of run-ins, but in here we were just like family, and on this day we stood side by side as though we'd risen together from the cradle.

"Kill my motha, Moe! On Big Face Gina, Texas Tech gonna handle that shit," Face shot back, and at this everyone busted out laughing.

"Mass, what's up with dat drink?" Boodah cut in.

"On the next move I'm supposed to meet the white boys in B-building. They got that white lighting down there. I got fifty books on me," I replied ready to party.

My fifty books of stamps totaled to $250.00 and was more than enough to get me and the crew twisted for the games. While I waited on the move, everyone continued placing their bets looking to bankrupt the bookie and claim ownership of being the prison's gambling guru.

"Yo, put this 2pk in real quick," I spoke to the bookie when the sound of feet shuffling spun me around in my seat. Scanning the area, the first thing that drew my attention was Boodah standing in the doorway of the upstairs laundry room. Instantly, I shot upstairs. As I approached, I could see the young homie, Fragle Rock, squaring up with a Memphis cat. As I entered they both stopped and looked in my direction. In my opinion, what was started had to be finished, so I nodded to continue and so they did.

Me, Boodah, Shine P, Face, Marty, and Lil' Head held down the door. Fragle Rock and Memphis went blow for blow, exchanging overhands and hooks alike. After about two minutes or so, we ended the fight and Boodah took Fragle Rock to his cell to clean him up. Fighting was normal in the pen. No weapons were drawn, so the minor blood spilled could easily be looked over.

A minute or two later, Memphis returned with one of his Florida homies. "Mass, y'all jumped my homie?" asked Florida.

Surprised by the accusation, but more offended by his approach, I stared him down. "Ain't nobody jump this nigga," I said, looking Memphis dead in his eyes.

An ass whipping was hard to swallow, yet both Memphis and Fragle Rock had equally got their thing off, so the lies about being jumped were frustrating, to say the least. Apparently, not satisfied with my response, Memphis and Florida headed towards Boodah's cell. When they arrived, we all arrived. Next came the knives, blood, fecal matter, and about a dozen or so inmates.

Punches were being thrown, knives being swung, and black eyes were being tossed out quickly. There was the sound of punctured flesh, people running, and others chasing. Rubber bullets were being shot by intervening staff, concussion bombs were being thrown, all the while C.O.'s were yelling. Afraid of what would happen if one stopped fighting, the fighting continued.

"Get on the ground!"

I was taken down by a few C.O.'s, a knee was rammed in my back, my arms were twisted, and my legs were shackled. Blood splatters were all over my clothes. Amid the pain of blows given and taken, there was a relief when it was all said and done. I could not have been happier to be alive. War was never friendly.

This time I knew I'd seen the last of Bloody Beaumont. I would've loved to have left on my way to a medium-security institution due to good behavior, but this was the way the cookie crumbled. Now I would have to sit in the hole and wait for my name to be called for a transfer to only God knows where.

While in the hole, everything had become numb. I felt nothing but failure. I understood that being by the side of your comrade when things hit the fan was a must, but when we got to Receiving and Discharge and we asked Fragle Rock what had kicked off the entire incident, I couldn't believe my ears. One book of stamps which was the equivalent of five dollars. Men were stuck inside the hole, others nearly lost their lives, and all for five measly dollars. The lot that was riding on my good behavior had been spoiled for a single book of stamps.

I thought about my children, my loved ones, and my current enrollment in college. This was either strained or over completely.

Remember my new beginning? Remember, I wanted it all to be over? That I was Massacre no more? Remember?

I beat myself up day and night, smothering my face in the pillow, banging my head on the bunk, and cried in the shower. On day one, SIS had come to my door making it clear that I was headed back to Pennsylvania, Lewisburg's Big House. That meant another two years in solitary, not counting my time here in the hole. I seriously doubted I would leave the SMU this go-round with many relationships intact.

That was the most crushing of blows. Prison shattered relationships. Combine this with stints of isolation where communication became less frequent, visits were stretched years apart, and your high school sweetheart ran off with her workplace confidant. Many had already begun losing faith in me. They figured I was not capable of leaving behind the things which led me to prison in the first place, and now that I was in this current predicament, I was beginning to question myself. This was all everyone needed to justify their departure. Five dollars! Selfish individuals disregarded what their greed would cost another. With respect to decision making, we oftentimes ignore the lives of those we love, and take actions which set everyone back.

****

February 2014

I was in transit headed back to the Big House. In case these solid truths of solitary confinement escaped you, in my stint in New Jersey State Prisons Management Control Unit back in 2003-2007 or the previous bit in Lewisburg, Allenwood 2010-2011, here we were again, 2014- until.

{*Solitary confinement and other forms of extreme isolation normally consist of 22-24 hour lockdown in a small cell. These terms often span anywhere from months, to years, or even decades. The United States Federal Bureau of Prisons holds over 10,000 individuals in 23 hours a day lockdown, making the Federal Government the largest practitioner of solitary, and other forms of isolated confinement, in the nation. Despite this considerable expense, the BOP remains unable to show how segregation practices enhance prison safety and public safety.*

Beyond fiscal considerations, the human costs of solitary confinement are well documented. Segregation units subject prisoners to dangerously low levels of physical and mental stimulation, endangering their mental health as well as their efforts towards rehabilitation. Studies demonstrate that even for the average person, experience of solitary confinement can result in a complete mental and emotional breakdown in as little as 48 hours. Individuals in isolation tend to experience physical and psychological degeneration from lack of regular human interaction.

When isolation lasts weeks, months, and years, prisoners experience physical and neurological changes as they become habituated to solitude, and often find it difficult, impossible even, to readjust to society upon re-entry. Not surprisingly, it is widely recognized that prisoners released directly from solitary units experience higher rates of recidivism.

Since 2015 the BOP has modified the governing policies of Special Management Unit as a means of reducing the consequences of isolation and the abusive environment. However, the new rules are unlikely to meaningfully improve human rights conditions.} (Brian Sonenstein of Solitary Watch)

This go-round, I thought about life and dreamed of death. I awoke on numerous days chilled and sweating uncontrollably. At times my eyes would open and I could see nothing. There was darkness everywhere and I could hear ghost-like murmurs. My train of thought was jaded. To myself, I would ask, *'Where am I?'* As familiar as the grounds were, I was trying to decipher the ins and outs. The inhumanness of such a terrible reality was confusing, to say the least. Before my arrival, I felt alive. Now I found it difficult to breathe. I was suffocating and escaping hope was all there was. The pain of it all was increasing daily. This time I was made aware of just how gripping the Federal Bureau of Prisons was.

It wasn't long after my arrival that my unit counselor arrived at my door informing me that my brother *'Beezo'* would be arriving from the SMU in Florence, Colorado where he'd been bidding for the last two years. In and out of trouble, the counselors felt it was a better fit that he be celled up with me. This was my younger brother; the same mother, same father, flesh and blood. The one whom I knew if my mother was forced to choose, she would most definitely want her *'baby'* to be home. Instead, he was with me.

I was serving a thirty year sentence, he was doing fifteen years. My mother had lost both of her sons. Still today I had to hide my feelings, and my emotions. I felt like I'd played a significant role in my brother's imprisonment and now I had to confront him head-on. I didn't know if I should be happy we would be reuniting after many years or if I should cry as a result of the pain it caused.

Upon his arrival, my brother was just as happy to see me, as I was to see him. We simply dismissed the pain of everything as many men do when it came to emotion. We simply went on about our time, never addressing the elephant in the room. We shared our 5 x 9 cell and discussed what his pending freedom would be like, my expectations, and his plans to get there and make the family proud.

For a solid ten months we did this, until it was my turn to leave. I was being sent to phase three of the program and he still had a few months before his level up. Did I cry? No! Did I want to? Maybe, but I'd dealt with this before; moving along while leaving behind another. It was never easy to deal with. As men, we cope, and we do our time. The struggle built bonds and when these bonds were broken in a physical sense, something tugged at the heartstrings.

"I'll see you later, Bro!"

****

Level Three.

I was paired up with my Beaumont crime partner, Shine P, out of South Carolina. He and I meshed good for our final ten months of the program. The end was right around the corner, so we worked out, and worked out some more. We celebrated when the unit counselor came to our door with our next designation spot. I was headed to USP McCreary in Kentucky, and Shine P was on his way to my old stomping grounds, USP Big Sandy. On the day of our departure, we both stayed up as long as we could. At 5 a.m. the officers were at our door demanding that we get ready. The feeling was one of elation and, I will be the first to tell you, I'd surely been kicked out of better places.

We went through the usual receiving and discharge process again for what seemed like the millionth time since I'd been locked up. Departing was similar to my first trip and took less than twenty inmates. It was obvious that not many made it out of Lewisburg. I smiled on the inside for the entire ride to the airlift, anticipating yet another grand escape from the clutches of confinement. Once on the plane, we were in the air amid a couple hundred other prisoners. Both men and women were being shipped across America. I just couldn't wait to get to where I was going.

****

Chapter 8

CHANGE WILL COME

My arrival at USP McCreary in Kentucky was one where I didn't know what to expect. Before leaving the SMU, there were a few comrades who were adamant in their testimony, saying I would be right back if I hit population chasing behind the same things I did before. This I knew, but what I didn't know was how to actually seek the change I had wanted for so long. It wasn't as easy as many thought in this environment. Most felt you said '*change*' and, like magic, it happened.

I had a lifetime of beliefs, be they right or wrong, and where to start was always the most difficult part to decipher. I was up to thirty-six years at this point; not days, not months, but years. I'd given up thirty years being committed to this way of life. So how do you say, '*I'm done*' and expect for there to be no roadblocks or setbacks? All this talk about new beginnings, the time was now to actually put my money where my mouth was, despite the costs. No longer could I put it off. Neither could I allow outside influences to pull me back.

The welcoming party at each prison played the same tune; care package, knife, and rules of engagement. A new arrival meant nothing more than a new excuse to justify walking around the compound like Rambo while professing to have changed. How would I get away? I couldn't run from my past; that was not an option. What could I do to attain the change I desired, without falling victim to the politics of prison or the ensnarement of old ways? I had to make this change.

What happened on the outside was not nearly as significant as what I needed to happen internally. My chase for the better had a lot to do with what I thought of myself. Did I feel that I was no more than a hustler or a gangbanger? Was I someone who wanted everything fast and easy or was I one who took pride in my ability to put in the necessary work for what I wanted? I was a man, thus my progression into manhood was one I had to welcome.

About a week or two after I'd arrived at USP McCreary, some fellow comrades of mine told me about a program I was familiar with, but dared not entertain, called the CHALLENGE PROGRAM. From what I knew, there would be snickering and frowning faces whenever someone mentioned the name of this program. The CHALLENGE PROGRAM was not in concert with the bad boy persona that was to be held in prison. The street code was: you stuck to the script, and despite the many examples of men and women in prison by a means of chasing the glitter and gold, you didn't waiver. If it meant prison or death, then that was what it was.

Challenging this obviously eroded way of thinking was cowardice. Nowhere in this world did a man want to be seen as weak amongst his peers, and so we behaved foolishly. It wasn't the CHALLENGE PROGRAM that was the problem, it was the betrayal of the code. *"I'mma die in these streets,"* was what many attested to. What came with the streets before being buried six feet deep? Cars, clothes, money, and, yes, prison. You could take it or leave it. Many couldn't leave it behind. I was no exception; that was until now.

The day I finally decided to enter the CHALLENGE PROGRAM, I remember standing in front of the doorway waiting to be let in. My palms were sweating as if I was on the verge of war. Maybe that was what this was: a war within my mind; an old way of life versus a new way. The instant the door opened I was caught off guard. What I'd known about prison did not exist here. I could see whites, blacks, and browns all sitting together at unit tables. There was music playing, reminding me of dollar night at the Patio's Lounge. The televisions were turned off, and everyone appeared to be in some sort of conversation. The most shocking was when an inmate approached me with his hand out.

"Good afternoon. Welcome to the CHALLENGE PROGRAM."

I was totally taken aback. Where this happened, I had no clue, but prison? Never! Segregation, separation, even assassination, but across the board togetherness amongst prisoners, even when forming against the administration, was unheard of. As prisoner after prisoner approached, expressing their pleasure in adding a new community member, my mind was simply drawing blanks. Unlike the Special Management Unit or the general population, this was a community of men leaving behind criminal behavior. Their actions displayed just as much.

I'd been told the program would last nine months and the treatment would be strenuous. The first twenty-four hours didn't change me. However, it did make me aware that change was possible.

The more I saw a lack of separation, and willingness to help, the more I believed. The threat of running popularity and swagger against modesty and maturity was lessening. For my entire life I had been married to the streets. Today I was feeling the freedom that accompanies divorce. I had stayed in an unhealthy relationship for over twenty years. As the days passed, I came to terms with what I needed and what was needed of me. Be it baby steps or one big 'Geronimo', I had to make a move.

Shortly after my arrival, I met with the treatment staff. My treatment specialist was one half of what we secretly within the community called 'Lavern and Shirley.' A pair of feisty, but fair, Caucasian women who paraded around the unit with a pure passion for change. Amongst the remaining treatment specialist was another relaxed Caucasian male counselor and an African American brother, who fancied we call him as none other than Dr. Booker.

The four treatment specialists grouped up and demanded the very best from everyone involved, though they all had unique ways of dealing with the community. When we'd basically felt we'd been counted out, they were giving us a chance. However, there were some days I found myself confused as I would witness inmate after inmate being expelled from the program.

Initially, I didn't understand. The program was about helping those who needed help. Snapping out of a criminal mind state didn't happen overnight. As the program went on, and the lessons began to hit me, the more I began to realize that change was a fragile process. Tolerating those who really didn't want to change could become detrimental to all involved. Still, I rooted for everyone and even found myself tutoring, and mentoring some of the program's population. I was utilizing my popularity as a tool to assist others in the same process I was part of.

As time went on, my treatment specialist, all five feet, one hundred and twenty pounds of her, would at times get on my case whenever she saw me backsliding. Tempers at times flared and she and I would end up having heated exchanges, or staying apart, giving one another room to cool off. This little lady was a bully with a positive push. Her counterpart was equally as gruesome. However, with the service of these two women, along with the two male specialists, I began to excel. I remember them telling me, '*If we can*

122

change you, we can change anybody'. Oh, so true. Though every now and then I'd drift out into the prison rec yard and find myself wrapped up in the penitentiary politics. Not that I didn't want to let go, just that I had yet to fully identify my triggers.

With prison as small as it was, once I became aware, it didn't mean that things would suddenly discontinue. Calling my name literally and figuratively were my comrades and trouble. *'You have a collect call from 25 to life! Pick up!'* Just as eager as I was to have Tamika, Tawanna, and Tamara answer my calls, I was equally as motivated to answer when penitentiary chances and six feet deep rang the alarm.

I was sliding out of the unit for a move or two, but whenever I got back, guilt would be plastered on my face. Over in the corner would be Lavern and Shirley. Never saying too much, but giving me the eye, which said it all. I couldn't escape these two for the life of me. Truthfully, they'd bet the house on me despite the cards being in criminality's favor. I could hit or miss, take their belief in me and leave them both bankrupted or I could double the wager by successfully completing the program and doing so honestly. I didn't want to disappoint these two women from rural Kentucky, so whenever I discovered myself slipping or annoyed with treatment, I would look down at their offices, think of all those who'd given up on me, and snap back.

Along with the help of my treatment specialist, I began to excel tremendously. By month six, I was nominated to become one of the program's official mentors. This was a feat that was unprecedented since a mentor first had to complete the entire program. I took this as a compliment and pushed even harder. I, along with the men within the community, saw the recognition of staff. We saw the belief in their eyes and began to look past the stereotypes and stigmas of the prison population, and collectively challenged one another to do better. The more we excelled, the more we challenged. Some of us fell short, relapsing to criminal behavior and substance abuse, just as some of us succeeded. Though trying, the Challenge Program gave me a clear view of what we as a people needed. Change!

****

Chapter 9

The Answer

It's 2017 and the new year had just begun. Nearly everyone was putting together their new year's resolutions or at least what I like to call the *'wish list'*. Lucky me, something *'new'* did transpire within my world. Following a continued clear conduct (incident free) stretch on my behalf, the Bureau of Prisons was finally *'freeing'* me from the clutches of the penitentiary and letting me step down to a lower level facility. After many failed attempts at stuffing me inside the Special Management Unit, despite my having no institutional infractions, I was seeing some form of relief. I was in my fifteenth year and the plethora of bumps, bruises, and broad beatings along the way was now hopefully behind me. I was tired of carrying prison-made knives for protection or peeking over my shoulder for a faceless enemy. Maybe, just maybe, this medium-security facility would offer me something new.

In February 2017, I was enroute to a federal correctional institution, Ray Brook, in upstate New York. Ray Brook, New York was only a few short hours from the soiled streets I'd fell in back in 2002. I sat in shackles moving side to side for nearly the entire bus ride, trying to ease the pain of tight cuffs cutting into my ankles and wrists. I was trying to contain the overwhelming feeling of fear within, which should have been excitement. I'd been away for so long, locked on the outskirts of the Atlantic and Mid-Atlantic regions, that I didn't recognize the route until the lights shone in the center of the darkness of the familiar territory. Until now the distance had awarded me an additional push when fighting the temptation which spilled from the pores of the New Jersey Turnpike.

New York, any part of it, prison or not, was placing me next door to everything I had learned since childhood. What lived here was everything that I knew I needed to stay away from. How would I manage? I hadn't been this close to Tewhan Jr. and my beautiful daughter Zamel since their breaths smelled of Similac, and each cried for the loving arms of a father figure. Prison for the past decade and a half prevented me from being present and providing the parental protection only a father could give. So as I transitioned from penitentiary to FCI, I also needed to convert from a prisoner to a parent.

I had been locked down in Louisiana, Texas, Kentucky, and Pennsylvania. All of these places gave me just enough leeway to be a "dad" during fifteen minute phone calls. However, when the phone beeped and the line went dead, so did our bond or a possible visit once a year over vending machine nothings, and card games of UNO, if the stars aligned.

Being so close to home would work wonders and do harm all at the same time. There was the threat of me relapsing, and returning to a place that raised me. Yet, this closeness awarded me the opportunity to be available for my children. What was more important? Over the years I'd met men in prison who cared little about being transferred to a medium-security prison. They felt that having a dangerous reputation (something that was afforded by doing time in a penitentiary) was far more important than being a father. They wished for their kids to mirror their ways and looked to them as role models, uncaring for the example being set. Ironically, this dangerous image and thug life modeling was doing nothing but leading one's children into the same cell where we lived.

Today, for me, the FCI wasn't about better housing. Prison was prison. A fenced-in college campus setting on a former Olympic training site, opposed to primeval penitentiary patterns did little to shift the conditional burdens of prison. Overall, this FCI was a step in the right direction of removing my children from the dangers of a world which cared little about a missing father.

This was the second semester of my hard-knock life, and comfortability wasn't a part of the curriculum. The penitentiary schooled me to the game. *'The rich get richer while the poor went to prison'.* I couldn't allow my children to end up here. For far too long prison had fractured the African American family structure. In the penitentiary, the correlation between prison and the poor bumped like bass drums. So my eyes weren't fixated on the fixtures surrounding me. I didn't see the filth of the place, the cubicle size cells, the ancient decor, or the pettiness of the staff trying their damndest to send me back to the penitentiary. The one thing I did notice on my first night in a two-man cell with a native New Yorker named 'X' was a typed document tacked to the corkboard of the cell.

'*Ubuntu!*' Its meaning blew my mind and reminded me that I was on the right track; that no part of my struggle was mine alone.

'*Ubuntu: I am because you are, because you are, therefore I am.*'

An anthropologist suggested to a group of young African tribe members to partake in a race where the winner would be rewarded with a basket full of fresh fruits. As the anthropologist gave the signal, the entire group held hands, ran the race in unison, bonded together, then sat and enjoyed the prize collectively. When asked why they had done such a thing when they were offered the possibility for one to be the winner, they replied, '*Ubuntu!*' How could one of us be happy while the rest was in despair? *"I am because we are."*

This brought back the time I spent in New Jersey State Prisons Management Control Unit over ten years ago, when fellow prisoner Massai Khaban offered me a care package and informed me his reason for doing so was, *"I am because you are."* Then, all I could see was the catchiness of the phrase and how I could utilize it in motivating the people of my gang, nothing more. I failed to see its true meaning and the powerfulness of such a statement, if lived by.

Today, after the many trials and errors of walking behind the wall and witnessing the damaging effects of individualism, the term meant everything. Surely we could rise from the troubles of the ghetto prisons, concentration camps, and penitentiaries if we bonded together and learned to live cooperatively. The time was allotted for one to reflect. Even on the outside, where we allow the wool to be pulled over our eyes, our plight was, in large part, the result of our own doing. It was our failure to recognize our strengths and weaknesses, and not capitalize on those strengths so that we can strengthen our weaknesses. We have to move beyond the limitations set by our oppressors.

'*Disaster or delight begins with self. The condition of a 'people' does not change until they first change themselves.*'

This wasn't fast talk or poetry in motion; this was truth. Prison was backbreaking. For that reason, this must be proof that we can stand up.

In large part, this was the beauty of prison. The time it allotted allowed one the chance to reflect. The closeness of the walls around me forced me to face reality. It encouraged me to inventory the emptiness and missing pieces that served to destroy me and my community. I was a father, and all around me lived fathers, brothers, and sons. All were pieces to a puzzle that could never be made whole until freedom became free for everyone. Not simply the lack of freedom by way of physical confinement, but also that of speech.

Many, like you and me, were residents of the graveyard and occupants of modern slave ships. Every minute of every day there was a man down because there was a culprit wielding a gavel, handing down life sentences like candy, fracturing families for generations. Imagine a baby being born, removed from daycare and turned over to your cities central booking; a baby's hand clutching a baby bottle, yet being shackled in cuffs. Can you imagine this? Sure you can! So fight!

****

At Ray Brook in 2017, I stood waiting for the ground to cave in, for the sky to fall or for something dramatic to happen. I had made it to the medium and nothing seemed the same. The prison had gotten me accustomed to certain things and in here things were nothing like it. The majority of those around me had handed over the '*life*' for something different, although they felt they were still honoring what once was. The culture had taken a backseat to tight shirts and fitted jeans. The lives lost were distant memories. What mattered here was what was trending. What I was seeing was showing me that my life was also changing. '*The life*' was changing.

A year in and there hadn't been any horrific acts of violence and, to be honest, I couldn't be happier. To pretend that I desired war was foolish. It appeared nearly ninety percent of the compound was looking for trouble. The search for trouble was a hunt for attention and nothing more, as when things heated up, they simmered just as quick.

In all honesty, the quiet was soothing. The tough pill to swallow was the lack of fight in the men around me, when it came to the system and the injustice thrown at us all. It was the blood, the sweat, and the tears of those who'd lost the battle, but refused to lose the war. The difference here was most had in and out bids, so they had become content with their time, simply happy not to be holed up.

One minute away from the world was too much, but the lack of consciousness clouded this fact. Every second counted and time was the last thing we wanted to be held up.

The hole was full, and the unit half empty. Everyone was glued to the television watching sports or FX. Most were upset that the cable company didn't provide VH1. Then a shift in the usual current of the prison came.

It was bus day and I was at my usual spot in the unit. Attentive as always, I scanned for incoming enemies. I waited and watched as the newcomers entered. New arrivals always gave off tell signs, though they didn't realize it. Fear resided in the windows of their souls, faux bravado spilled from their pores, and the scent was detectable from far. Some tiptoed, unafraid to display their fear, but on this bus day, there was one.

His walk was different and held a certain confidence. To him, I would have to pay close attention. He was in his early 40's, stood about 5'6, and had stocky build. I could tell that he'd been around. An enemy I didn't call it, but he was someone who potentially held a key to another realm of reality. Unwilling to award too much credit, I would have to wait and see. The fact that he'd been around let me know his every move was a calculated one. It would be like playing chess. A pawn pushed, a castle surrendered, then checkmate!

It wasn't twenty minutes following his arrival the calculated move happened. He took his shirt off at the back of the unit and began to do sets of pull-ups. This was an action that was taken in an attempt to exert dominance and strength. So soon? Though this may have gone unnoticed by the remainder of the unit, I was well aware. This move was what he wanted everyone to see, yet I saw more. Physical strength jaded the minds of those who believed power erupted from the pressure applied to biceps and triceps. From a distance I played it cool. I just relaxed and observed. Even though I needed to pay close attention to all, this particular individual stood out a bit more. After a few months I learned that the new arrival's name was M.C.

M.C. had been in prison for the past twenty years. He had been holding it down for all five New York boroughs and was soon to depart to regain all of what had been stolen him years ago: his legacy. Like us all when sentenced, the threat of generational continuity was present. M.C. found himself in a hurry to return to the outside; his family depended on it. Similar to myself, he came in at the tender age of twenty-two and grew up under the ranks of true warriors. It was men of his stature who I chose to learn from, gather information, and multiply my development.

With experience being the best teacher, who could deny that a twenty-two year veteran had a collage of experiences. Did I need to touch the stove to know it was hot or could I adhere to the gifts awarded by those before me? Through mutual acquaintances, M.C. and I began speaking on occasions and as our conversations grew, we recognized our shared struggles. Furthermore, I learned that M.C. appreciated art, music, poetry, and the pursuit of knowledge. During our conversations, he would tell me to, "*keep fighting, never to give up*, and *stay solid.*"

Along the course of one of the first exchanges we had, he let on that he too had been paying attention. It was true that strength recognized strength. He told me about the many differences he'd seen in the feds, and how today there was little to no respect for the game. Indeed, this was true. The fact that the many playing had begun to change the rules helped in my decision to walk off into the sunset a lot sooner, leaving behind the self-destructive way of life I'd once believed was everything. There was no denying my conviction to change. However, when I arrived at Ray Brook I was instantly reminded of the Lil' Hip Hop's, Kwame's, and the Too Kool's of my neighborhood. Before I knew it, I was center stage.

The majority of the homies on the compound were in their early to mid-twenties and looked at myself, and a few others, for guidance. The guidance they were in search of had nothing to do with freedom or change, but everything to do with how to become more aggressive. The more I socialized, walking the track with the homies and working out with the homeboys, the deeper I found myself falling once again. I loved the '*life*' so whenever the '*life*' and I came face to face, I gave up little resistance.

The youth around me made me feel alive or so I thought. The once good-natured stories they would share with me quickly turned into bickering, and internal gripes, each looking for me to choose a side. The '*life*' was bending to geographic's, the way was crumbling to individualism, and the loud noise hurt my heart. Everybody wanted to kill everybody, especially one another. The camaraderie and the brotherly love were gone. The universal oneness that once brought everyone together was removed. The sight of it all made me want to give more and to repair the damage. Then I was passed a book and the first chapter jumped out at me immediately. *'Helping others by hurting yourself'*.

I couldn't believe it. My entire life I felt sacrifice was the way to go, even if it meant giving up all of myself. Thoughts shared with me about loyalty as a two-way street meant nothing to me. They wanted you to give, give, and give some more or die trying. If you stopped giving then you were a traitor.

At thirty-seven I had to learn how to be loyal to me and mine. The acknowledgment of such, along with maturation, led me to Jummah. I needed help. I needed more than the Challenge Program. I needed more than female companionship. I needed something to salvage my soul. I walked into the folds of Islam and took a leap of faith. Proud that I had made the conscious decision to bring about a better me, M.C. stopped me in the unit, pulled me to his cell and shared the following.

"Listen, baby bro. It's extremely imperative for you to know how to properly navigate through, not only this prison system, but the hellish conditions that exist within these walls. In order to survive this psychological warfare, one must be able to use the intellectual dynamics of their mind. You can do this by constantly feeding your mental state of being with positive images, literature, and things that will allow you to grow healthy."

"Take advantage of the education and learn as much as you can. Pick up a trade, stay busy, and ultimately, stay sucka free. By doing all the above you won't fall victim or be plagued with the negative energies of ignorance that so often weakens one's thought processes. Not only for you, but for your family and loved ones who are on the other side waiting for your safe return. When you suffer, they suffer."

"The name of the game is mastery of self. In doing so you'll not only master everything outside of self, but you'll never be mastered by others again, overstand? In acquiring this knowledge, wisdom, and understanding of one's self, you'll be able to free yourself from the psychological bondage that we so often forget exists due to the physical realm of conditional distraction, that keeps you held captive from not knowing your true value and worth, which in return blocks you from reaching your full potential."

"Let me ask you a question? What do you hope to accomplish during your long journey throughout this course, which inturn blocks you from reaching your full potential? Because I'm telling you what these people have in store for you. They got a whole lot of hatred, pessimism, and anything else that'll stifle you and your greatness. Now that's some deep shit, right? But it's real! So I feel it's my duty and responsibility, from one warrior to another, to prevent such atrocities. But at the end of the day, it's up to you."

"As a twenty-one year veteran of this system, who studied the structural dynamics of this prison industry, I hope you take heed to my loving advice. Because only love and respect speak with the tongues of truth. With that said, anything I can ever assist you with to foster your growth and development, know I got you."

With that said, we both went back to our day as if the words he'd just spoken weren't strong enough to shake the ground. This was the last conversation M.C. and I had the pleasure of having. Shortly thereafter, the prison was locked down, and M.C. was released after serving twenty one and a half years. Understanding the blessing of having such a knowledgeable brother around, I set out to write to M.C., but I have yet to send it. Being M.C. may never get the letter, I shall share it with you all.

****

M.C.

Peace comrade. I know it took a while for me to get at you. However, I wanted to let all of what you had given me marinate within my soul. It took a second to digest the many jewels you shared, and with my mind's eye, I'll one day be able to digest it all. Even knowing prison for what it is, I still can't imagine the trials and tribulations you've endured in the span of 21 years, for each journey is unique. Had it not been for myself being a 17-year vet at this stage I would have continued viewing survival and its means as just another day.

Survival never would've been seen in regards to lockdowns, solitary, hunger strikes, hot as hell days, and freezing cold nights. Survival would not have meant enduring the abuse of authority, cell extractions, and whole men being broken into fractions. It never would have translated into rejected phone calls, unanswered emails, denied visits, cheating wives, and disloyal friends.

On this side, we survive betrayal, deceit, resentment, calls of crying children, and weeping mothers. Let's not forget the brother who doesn't know how to keep.

We survive miseducation, stolen legacies, Jim Crow laws, reinvented slavery, racial injustice, and judicial genocide.

We endured black booted stomp outs, razor-sharp knives, locks in socks, and peanut butter and knuckle sandwiches. Then there were the failed GED math quizzes, parenting classes, money-smart courses, discontinued college curriculums, and substance abuse counseling. We survived medicated poison, self-medicated intoxicants, and physical act right.

Yet, we're surviving. The remedy for prison, there is none. The methods and strategies that come in sets of 33 do not apply within these walls. You meet adversity head-on, keep your head up, and chest out.

Comrade, a while back I was asked a question and I could find no articulate wordplay or intellectual response. Now with your help, I am finally able to answer.

How do I survive prison?

The answer... I just do!

Epilogue

The toughest, most trying times were those spent on the inside of prison. The outside world moving at its own pace and marching at its own drum, worried not of the trouble we endured. Those who do worry were unsure of how to help, so they ignored it. Your experiences cannot be put into words, your pain unable to be related to, and your death would be a lonely one. But why me? A question asked by millions, meaning there were millions on the inside. Millions that were suffering in solitary. Millions attempting to hold on to a life which had been snatched when sentenced. Millions alone! Alone, yet accompanied by millions more.

If I stood shackled in conjunction with millions, how was I alone? Maybe, just maybe, I was alone as a consequence of being faceless… nameless. There were 2.2 million invisible men and women whose pain was pleasure to a system designed to punish. But weren't we deserving of punishment? Commit the crime, do the time; open and shut, case closed. The in-between, the beginning, the end, pivotal; make them, no… make us suffer.

The callousness of every 24 hours etched into the stint of 360 months. Time! Eyes wide open, legs moving, emotions gone, and the pain was excruciating. Nothing but darkness and 360 months of blank space. Time never to be regained. What was left? Your life melting into a mixture of nothingness buried deep inside. Then there was a moment I began to believe from nothing came something. That the system had a flip side, a hidden compartment.

The prison didn't open its doors, yet it did welcome in a chance to transform my tragedy into triumph. The college classes began to chill that which was once a rising temper. I was being provided purpose and offered solace. I was building with the college professors the freedom of judgment, homework, class projects, and a new world. I was amazed by the beauty of brilliance. Then it happened. I was told that when someone showed you who they were, believe them. I was indeed reminded of the cold, unforgiving nature of the system. I was reminded that freedom for some was a privilege and not a right.

I was working towards an Associates Degree in Social Science, preparing myself for a brighter future with an angel on my right shoulder whispering, *"You can do it"*. I was seizing the opportunity, and that in itself represented success. I was proudly placing my pencils and pens in my school bag, double checking my Math 120 assignments, and typing essays for English 12. I began doing what I had never thought and what they themselves couldn't believe. The looks on the faces of my loved ones when I would tell them, *"I did it!"* pushed me everyday down the hill to the school building. The looks on the faces of the disbelievers equally as encouraging.

"Look at me now, world!"

****

It was April 16, 2019 and I was going over notes for our upcoming final. My notebooks were sprawled across my desk while I heard my fellow prisoners passionately discussing the authenticity of love. My semester GPA was a 3.5. Must I remind you I was doing it! That's when it happened!

"Butler!" shouted the school teacher. The feeling in the pit of my stomach told me something was wrong. Five minutes later I stood inside the holding tank of the L.T.'s office as they informed me that I was to be placed in the hole under SIS investigation. Back to the hole I went, unsure how to process yet another setback. I instantly drew back. The joyous feeling of success vanished in an instant. The smiles I envisioned on the faces of my loved ones turned into frowns.

Had I created a presence so powerful that even when I sought to shift, the change was unbelievable? My evolution was not televised. What they did not know left them swimming in ignorance. No one could tell me not to believe the system didn't hate what it didn't understand. Evidence? Reasoning? There were none. The means which conveniently justified *'their'* end whenever *'I'* was moving forward was, *"Butler's influence. Butler's a leader!"* But what did Butler do? The answer? A hidden treasure never found, yet the illusion would suffice. What I did to be in prison was reason enough to serve me countless sentences whenever I showed any signs of change. On July 25th, 2019, I was shipped again. It was my eighth transfer in seventeen years.

ABOUT THE AUTHOR

Tewhan Butler is the 2016 *In The Margins* top non-fiction award winning author of **Americas Massacre: The Audacity Of Despair And A Message Of Hope**. He is a certified substance and alcohol abuse counselors trainee, a written contributor to Prison Insiders inside/outside project, the CEO of Interstate Icon Clothing (ig@interstateicon), and Co-Chairman of the publishing company Interstate Inkmanship. **Americas Massacre: Surviving Mass Incarceration** is Butler's second book.

To Contact Author:
Emai: interstateinkmanship@gmail.com
Text: 216-304-8257
Write: Tewhan Butler #26852-050@bop.gov

www.ingramcontent.com/pod-product-compliance
Lightning Source LLC
Chambersburg PA
CBHW060612200326
41521CB00007B/748